How to Talk So People Will Listen

Steve Brown

BakerBooks
Grand Rapids, Michigan

© 1993 by Steve Brown

Published by Baker Books
a division of Baker Publishing Group
P.O. Box 6287, Grand Rapids, MI 49516-6287
www.bakerbooks.com

Paperback edition published in 1999
Audio version available

Sixteenth printing, December 2008

ISBN 978-0-8010-6144-8

Printed in the United States of America

The Library of Congress has cataloged the hardcover edition as follows:
   Brown, Steve, 1940—
      How to talk so people will listen / Steve Brown.
         p.   cm.
      ISBN 10: 0-8010-1057-8
      ISBN 978-0-8010-1057-6
      1. Communication—Religious aspects—Christianity
      2. Communication. I. Title
   BV4319 .B76 1993
   248.4—dc20   92042235

Scripture is taken from The Holy Bible, New King James Version, copyright ©1979, 1950, 1982 by Thomas Nelson, Inc., Publishers

Contents

Introduction

Henry Clay was a speaker of great acclaim. If you are successful at anything, those who aren't successful will be jealous. Some of the older members of the house were jealous of Clay's ability to sway a crowd with his speeches, and one of them said to him in a rather snide way, "Your problem, Henry, is that you speak for the immediate impact on your audience. I speak for posterity."

"Yes," Clay replied, "and it seems that you are willing to keep talking until the arrival of your audience."

In other words, Clay was saying that his critics were people who talked without anybody listening. Their audience was not a real one. This is (hopefully) a practical book about normal, everyday people talking to normal, everyday people. It is not a book for scholars or professional communicators. It is, in short, a book written to help you reach a real audience—the one we encounter every day of our lives.

Have you ever made a fool of yourself in a public speech? Have you ever wondered what to say next in a conversation with a friend or acquaintance? Have you ever seen speakers sway a crowd and thought that you would like to be able to do that? Have you ever wondered why your words had no effect on the people who heard them? Have you ever felt ignored in a conversation, at a party or behind a podium? Have you ever wished you could improve your speaking and conversation skills? Have you ever given a report and found that nobody understood what you reported or didn't even care? Have you ever wished you could say things to your employees that would motivate them toward more efficient work, or wished you could say something to your boss that would motivate him or her toward giving you a raise?

If you've had those wishes, this book is for you.

It's a book about talking.

I'm a talker and a reasonably successful one. This book isn't going to be filled with academic jargon or impractical theory. The information has come from a lifetime of trial and a whole lot of error. The best way to learn to do something is to first do it wrong, and I've done it wrong a lot. I'm going to give you an opportunity to learn from my failure and success.

I teach communications at Reformed Seminary where I try to help young preachers get the fire to the front pew. I spend a considerable portion of my time speaking at conventions, churches, colleges, and seminars. Currently I speak on a daily fifteen-minute radio program heard on over three hundred stations across the country. I have worked in commercial broadcasting, selling everything from Cadillacs to cigarettes, and in Christian broadcasting with a far better message. As the host of a "Christian talk show," I spend a lot of time discussing people's problems with a view to helping them find some answers.

In other words, my job is talking. (Of course, it is far more than that, but, at minimum, it is what I do for a living.) Talking is the train that carries the product to the market. The product may be the best any industry has to offer, but if there is no transportation to get it to the public, then the best product in the world will remain on the shelves.

I'm a Christian and I have a concern that Christians learn to talk better. I'm not afraid that the Christian message suffers from lack of truth. It really is true! I'm afraid that it suffers from talkers who don't know how to talk. As part of my personal calling, I want to help my Christian family talk better.

But communication skills are amoral (they are either effective or ineffective, not "good" or "bad"). So, if you are a pagan, this book might help you too. Just don't tell anybody where you got the information.

The major problem with talking is that everybody does it, yet hardly anybody understands what it does and how it affects others. In any given day, you will have heard thousands upon thousands of words spoken by a whole lot of people. The odds are that you won't remember what most of those words communicated. Not only that, during any given day you will speak thousands of words, and few people will even understand or remember what your words communicated.

I'm writing this book to fix one side of that equation: *your* side. I want you to talk better, to talk so people will listen.

Mostly, I want you to talk better so that your words will make a difference in your church, or your family, or your business or with your friends.

But, also, maybe I'll meet you someday. Perhaps I'll hear you make a speech or preach a sermon. Maybe we will talk. And, to be painfully honest with you, I want to enable you to talk better so that I won't be bored to tears when we meet.

1

The Power of Speech

For by your words you will be justified, and by
your words you will be condemned.
Matt. 12:37

Have you ever wondered what it would be like to lose the power of speech? You couldn't communicate quickly or easily with others about your needs, your feelings, or your desires. You wouldn't be able to correct false impressions or share your ideas. You couldn't encourage or reprimand or inspire. You wouldn't be able to express anger or love or joy. If you couldn't talk, you would be forced into the shell of your private world and it would be a lonely place indeed.

I was speaking at a conference in Detroit and, for the first time in my life, developed a bad case of laryngitis. The only way I could speak was in a whisper and with the sound system turned up very loud. And the only way I could do that was to refrain from talking to anybody outside of the public time on the platform.

Frustrating? You have no idea. I realized then how much I depend on speech. Things I take for granted, like saying "good morning" or ordering a meal in a restaurant, weren't possible. There could be no dinner conversation, no way to respond to questions. Worst of all, I couldn't call home in the evening and talk to my wife. I found myself becoming quite depressed and angry. The most frustrating thing about it was that I couldn't tell anyone how frustrated and angry I really was.

We never realize how important something really is until we lose it. At that conference I discovered how much we depend on words. Language is one of the most important gifts human beings possess. Entire civilizations can trace their beginnings to the point where their speech became viable. "Civilized" is often defined by anthropologists in terms of speech. Most of our early childhood memories go back to that precise time when we first learned to speak. Learning the language of a culture or a country is the most important factor in being successful in that culture.

The problem with many people is that they have taken the gift God has given and have wasted it. I have a friend who used to comment (when there was still a Soviet Union) that there wasn't much difference between the United States and the Soviet Union in the area of free speech. He said, "In the Soviet Union they don't have freedom of speech, and they don't say anything. In America we have freedom of speech, and we don't say anything either. So what's the difference?" He was saying that freedom of speech doesn't mean anything if you don't have anything to say.

Many people live frustrated lives because they haven't learned how to use speech properly. They either have nothing to say, or say it so poorly that nobody cares when they do say it. What a pity.

You say, "Steve, come on. I realize that you talk for a living and you think speech is important. But haven't you overestimated the importance of speech? There are lots of more important things. My frustrated life, when it is frustrated, has a lot to do with many things—but one of them isn't speech."

Let's talk about it.

Words have power, you know.

When God speaks, His very speaking accomplishes the purpose of His words. "So shall My word be that goes forth from My mouth; it shall not return to Me void, but it shall accomplish what I please, and it shall prosper in the thing for which I sent it" (Isa. 55:11). In the Bible, words are often used to accomplish their purpose, thus there are "benedictions" (blessings) and "maledictions" (curses) which have the power to bless or destroy. Jesus said that we would be either justified or condemned by our words. It is no accident that the incarnation was described in John 1 as the "Word becoming flesh." When God wanted to punish Zacharias because of his unbelief, He took from him the power to speak.

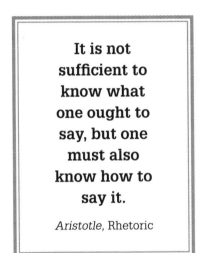

It is not sufficient to know what one ought to say, but one must also know how to say it.

Aristotle, Rhetoric

Words Can Bless

I teach students at the seminary that it is desperately important that they affirm the congregations they serve. Too many pastors feel they have been sent to a church to preach the wrath of God, to straighten out the members, and to fix all the problems. The truth is that God usually calls a pastor to a church to love its people and to tell them so.

There is a correlation of what I teach at the seminary to other areas too. For instance, a number of years ago a friend of mine asked for my help with the problems he was having in his business. I asked him if he ever told the people who worked for him that he appreciated and valued them. He replied that he paid them and felt that this was enough. "Steve," he said, "every time I give them a paycheck, I've affirmed them."

My mother may have had an ugly child, but not a dumb one. My friend thought his problems had to do with laziness in his employees. That wasn't the problem, as any nitwit could see. After I taught my friend some of the things I'm going to teach you in this book, the change was radical and astounding. He told me later, "Who would have believed that something that little could make a difference that big?"

When I think of people who have made a difference in my life, I remember those who have used their words to encourage, motivate, and affirm me. I think of the five retired pastors in the little church on Cape Cod who had the power to destroy the young pastor in their midst. Instead, they decided among them that they were going to be my cheerleaders. Time after time, when I was discouraged and ready to quit, those godly men would speak words of comfort and love. I often think of what would have happened to my ministry and my life if those men had decided to "fix" me with their words.

My friend and colleague R. C. Sproul, one of the most prolific and insightful Christian writers in America, was once told by a schoolteacher, "R. C., Don't let anyone ever tell you that you can't write." Her words became a motivating factor in the writing of his books.

I read three or four books a week and can't imagine what life would be like if I couldn't read. I love reading because an eighth-grade teacher encouraged me to read and then taught me how.

When Sir Walter Scott was a boy he was not considered very bright. As a result, most folks ignored him. When he was twelve, he went to a social gathering where a number of literary figures were present.

Robert Burns, the famous Scottish poet, was admiring a painting under which was written a couplet of poetry. He asked about the author but nobody knew who had written the lines. That was when Scott very shyly gave the author's name and quoted the rest of the poem. Burns placed his hand on the young boy's head and said, "Son, you will be a great man in Scotland someday."

Years later, Scott remembered Burns' encouraging words as the turning point in his life. They made the difference between a man settling for a life of obscurity or reaching for greatness.

Wives and husbands don't often realize how important they are in the success and failure of their spouse's career and relationships. My wife, Anna, has always been a benediction on my life. Oh, she is loved by her husband for a number of reasons. She is beautiful and fun. She has been a wonderful mother. She is a great cook. Her abilities in business and in management are superb. But the most important gift she has given me over all the years of our marriage has been the fact that she believed in me—and told me so. She has picked up the pieces of a sermon that bombed or a project that failed and has applied the words of encouragement and affirmation that enabled me to get up each time I was knocked down.

Words Can Destroy

There is a rhyme many of us learned about words: "Sticks and stones may break my bones, but words can never hurt me." I suspect my mother taught me that rhyme when someone had said something cruel and hurtful to me. She wanted me to know that I could survive the verbal onslaught of thoughtless people. I'm sure it helped, but she was wrong.

Words can hurt far more than sticks and stones. In fact, much of the pain and sorrow with which we all live comes from words. Words used as a curse can destroy us. If you don't believe me, think of those incidents in your life when someone's words devalued you ("If brains were dynamite, you wouldn't have enough to blow yourself out of a peanut shell!"), or when angry words stung so terribly that you thought you would die ("You are a stupid idiot! I can't believe you did that!"), or when critical words eliminated the possibility of success, ("Can't you ever do anything right? Look at how you bungled it!"), or when words let you know that you weren't important, ("Here's a quarter. Go call someone who cares!").

Query: "Has he finished his speech yet?"

Response: "He finished long ago. He just won't quit talking!"

Bill Glass, who works with prisoners, often asks at his meetings in prisons, "How many of you had a father or mother who told you something like, 'Son, some day you are going to end up in jail'?" Bill says that time after time almost all of the prisoners raise their hands affirming the prophetic power of their parents' words.

Our children often become what we *say* they will become. If we tell them they are stupid, they will probably act that way. If we tell them that they won't amount to anything, they probably won't. If we speak to them like criminals, they will, in all probability, become criminals. While physical and sexual abuse of children is horrible and rampant in our society, verbal abuse, while it is not often recognized and condemned as such, can be almost as devastating.

One of the key principles of business management is that words of encouragement or discouragement affect production. Leaders have great power to destroy, discourage, and debilitate their followers with words. How many times have teachers demolished a potential Einstein with thoughtless words? Think of the marriages that have been destroyed, the friendships shattered, the churches divided because of careless words.

Words Define How We See Ourselves

Words do more than bless and curse. The words you use when you are talking define how you think about yourself. Give me a few minutes of conversation with almost anyone and I'll be able to tell you whether that person thinks of himself or herself as a champion or a chump.

John Wesley, after some significant failure in his life, became convinced that faith was the key to reaching the world for God, but had trouble making faith a reality in his life. He went to one of his mentors and asked this question: "How can I preach faith if I don't have faith?"

Wesley's mentor made an interesting comment. "Mr. Wesley," he said, "preach faith until you have faith, and then because you have faith you will preach faith." In other words, "Learn to see yourself as a man of faith, articulate that reality in your life, and then you will become a man of faith." Words do define how we see ourselves and determine, sometimes, what we become.

I want to show you how to begin to think more highly of yourself and to articulate that reality to others. You will be surprised at the power of words to change your life. There are some people whose conversation and speaking style could be described as a perpetual whine. In their talking they have defined what they think of themselves, which leads me to the next point.

Words Set the Parameters of How People Will React to You

If your verbal messages sound like a perpetual whine, you must expect that people will treat you accordingly. If you speak with authority, people will react to you as a person with authority. If you speak words of love, people will react to you with love. If your words reflect a seething anger, don't be surprised if people avoid you except when they want to fight you or enlist you in their battles with someone else.

Religious people can sometimes be quite pompous. Not too long ago I was criticized quite harshly in a church magazine for something I had said. I received letters from all over the country in which people tried to correct my "spurious theological views." But by far the most interesting feedback in that whole episode came from a quite stiff and religious young man who approached me after I had spoken at a conference. He said, "Dr. Brown, what you said grieved my heart." (Watch it when Christians say their "heart is grieved." That generally means they have a howitzer pointed at you and are getting ready to pull the trigger.)

I said to the young man, "Son, this is a small conference held in a small place and I'm a peon. There isn't anything here big enough to grieve your heart."

> **If the minds of men were laid open, we should see but little difference between that of the wise man and that of the fool. The difference is that the first knows how to pick and cull his thoughts for conversation . . . whereas the other lets them all indifferently fly out in words.**
>
> *Joseph Addison*

He was shocked and then spoke about his concern for me. "Don't you want to hear what a brother in Christ has to say?"

"No, son," I replied, "I really don't, unless you want to spit it out. I've had about enough spiritual nonsense for one day. If you want to tell me what you really *think*, without all the subtle trappings, I will listen."

"I think," he almost shouted, "that you are arrogant and rude!" And then he started blushing. It was probably the first up-front and honest thing he had said in a long time.

"I think," I said, "that I agree with you. But I am better than I was and God isn't through with me yet." Then we began to talk, and it turned out to be a very pleasant and helpful exchange.

His opening words, however, set the parameters of what was clearly going to be an adversarial relationship. He didn't mean to do that. He just didn't realize that words often determine how people react to people.

When I was in commercial broadcasting and part of the news team of a radio station in Boston, I learned that if one can't pronounce a word correctly, one should mispronounce it with boldness and people will think *they* are wrong. If your conversations are always reflecting "Harry's humble habit," you will find that people will assume that you have every reason to be humble. (As the psychiatrist said to the patient, "The reason you have an inferiority complex is because you *are* inferior.") If you reflect confidence in your message (whether that is a sales talk, a presentation of the gospel, a sermon, or an acceptance speech), you will inspire confidence in your hearers. If you apologize for what you are about to say ("I don't tell stories very well, but I heard the funniest joke the other day. . ." or "I am not a public speaker but . . .") people will think that you have much about which to apologize.

The words you use will determine your success or failure in accomplishing the goal you set when you speak the words.

I was once the pastor of a church where it became necessary to add some new buildings. We were told that the new buildings would cost no more than one and a half million dollars. The lowest of five bids from contractors was over three million. In trying to explain the building program to the members, we almost junked the whole program. The building committee resigned and a blanket of doom settled over the leadership.

I called a friend of mine who had been through three building programs and told him my problems. (There is something weird about any pastor who has gone through more than one building program. One building program is a result of inexperience. Anything more reflects a warped personality.) He gave me two pieces of valuable advice. First, he told me that a leader must lead. And second, he told me that once I had laid the first brick, the problems would stop.

I called two guys and had them report to me. I told them that in two weeks we were going to have a ground-breaking ceremony in the parking lot. "I don't know what we are going to build," I added. "It may be only an outhouse . . . but we are going to build something." Then I called my pastor friend and said, "Jim, if you are wrong, I'm in serious trouble."

Over the next few months I spoke words of encouragement and vision to that congregation. At times I was discouraged and without vision, but I continued to use the words that were needed. The congregation was too small to build such elaborate buildings and a number of people left the church and there were times when I would pray, "Lord, are you sure you want this thing built?"

You know something? Those buildings are now standing. The congregation is proud of what has been accomplished. People who, before the building started, had said, "We can't do this. It's too big and we are too little," are now saying, "Look what we did!" They are pleased at what God did with people who were committed to a project. And most of all, there is one amazed preacher (me) who still looks back to those days with unbelief. It is hard to believe, sometimes, how God uses words of vision to inspire a people to do what they thought was impossible.

Do words have power? Of course they do.

Rabbi Stephen Samuel Wise was asked to address an anti-Nazi meeting in Brooklyn. As a result of his acceptance, he received a number of threatening letters. Some of the writers told him he would be killed if he addressed the rally. When the day finally came, Wise mounted the podium and said this: "I have been warned to stay away from this meeting under pain of being killed. If anyone is going to shoot me, let him do it now. I hate to be interrupted."

Now *there* was a man who knew the power of words! He had something to say, knew how to say it, and dared anybody (others knew the power of words too) to try to stop him.

Do words have power? Give me ten men or women like Rabbi Wise and I can change the world.

2

Dealing with
the Intimidation Factor

"But when they deliver you up, do not worry about
how or what you should speak. For it will be given
to you in that hour what you should speak."
Matt. 10:19

It was late in the evening when I got the call. The woman
who called was the president of a rather large and prominent religious organization with a feminist agenda.

"Steve," she said, "sorry to call so late, but I've been
putting it off. I have something to ask you, but I'm afraid
to ask."

"Go ahead," I replied, "and as the male half of this conversation, fulfilling his male role of providing answers for
women, I will give you an answer."

"Steve," she continued, not sure I was joking, "I don't
need any information, I need a speaker for our church
group. Would you do it?"

I accepted the invitation and then, puzzled, asked her why she was afraid. In a rare burst of honesty, she said, "Because you intimidate me." In a rare burst of returned honesty, I said, "That's funny. I thought it was the other way around." The background of that conversation can be found in a number of meetings that both of us had attended. On those occasions, her strong feminist agenda and her vocal advocacy of feminist causes created a situation where I didn't know how to respond. So I responded with veiled hostility. Whenever she would leave the room, I would jump up from my chair and open the door for her. I made a point of always helping her on with her coat. If we were in a debate, I always sat down and "let" her speak first because that was a man's responsibility: to give way to the "fairer and weaker sex." I made a point of complimenting her on the way she looked when I knew she wanted me to compliment her on what she thought or said.

The reason I reacted to my friend that way was because she—her ability, her intellectual prowess, her strong personality—intimidated me. It was a source of amazement for me to discover that *I* intimidated *her*. I suspect that she was as surprised as I was.

One of the major problems in communication whether personal or public, is the intimidation factor—when poor communication takes place because one or both of the parties is intimidated. But more important, for the purposes of this chapter, the intimidation factor causes most potential speeches to fail to make it to the first row, and many personal conversations to be stifled before they get started.

What does one do about the intimidation factor?

Do people frighten you? Do you refuse to speak in public because the experience is just too traumatic? Do you find yourself reacting to someone else's anger with silence and fear? Have you ever tried to present your ideas to another person only to find yourself stammering and unable to get your ideas together? Do you find that you never disagree with anyone about anything because you are afraid that people will think that you are stupid? Do you avoid certain people because you think they are especially important or intelligent? Does your mouth go dry at the very thought of giving a report at a business meeting? Does your hand start trembling whenever you are called on to respond publicly to a question in class? Do you avoid small groups because you are afraid you will be noticed and will have to say something?

If you answered yes to any of the above questions, you are a victim of the intimidation factor, and I'm going to help you. In fact, because this is the most critical problem in the area of communication, this will be the longest chapter in the book. Don't skip it. It's important.

You see, most people who have a communication problem believe that the problem is their technique, when it really is their terror of other people. Over and over again, when I try to help people communicate better, I discover that, even with the proper technique and an adequate vocabulary, they are still terrible communicators. Why? Because the problem wasn't in something they needed to learn, but something they needed to feel.

This is the plan: We will wake up and examine some of the "dogs" of intimidation and then, one by one, we'll "shoot those suckers."

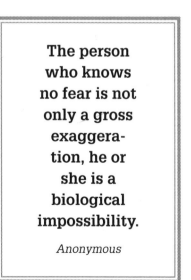

The person who knows no fear is not only a gross exaggeration, he or she is a biological impossibility.

Anonymous

Apprehension Intimidates

First, let's talk about the intimidating power of apprehension.

This is when we make the mistake of crossing a bridge before we are even close to the river. In other words, we create an imaginary picture in a communication situation where we say or do something quite stupid and embarrassing. It involves the fear of shame and the nightmare of showing one's inferiority.

Often, in marriage counseling, I encounter this form of the intimidation factor, and it can kill a marriage. Usually in a marriage one person is confrontational, and the other is not; one person likes to get issues out on the table and solved, and the other would rather just ignore problems with the fond hope that they will go away. It has nothing to do with one's gender. Sometimes the confrontational person is the woman and sometimes the man. It's just that one person is verbal and the other is not. The verbal and confrontational person wins all the arguments, expresses all the opinions, and makes all the decisions.

It doesn't take a brain surgeon to understand that if a marriage goes on very long under that kind of rubric, the marriage will get into serious trouble. There is often agreement, but that's only another name for "submission."

I have spent considerable time teaching couples how to bring balance to that situation. I teach the confronter how to back off to encourage his or her spouse to express opinions, engage in arguments, and make decisions. I encourage the other spouse to speak up, even when afraid, and to stand his or her ground, even if it is uncomfortable ground. A few simple elements of assertiveness training can often make a big difference in a marriage.

The interesting thing, however, about spouses who are non-confrontational is that they almost always have a self-image that *expects* failure and shame. In other words, the

person who won't confront is, more often than not, a person with a mental picture painted by failure and guilt.
It is not my purpose to engage in a psychological or theological discussion on how to deal with a poor self-image. (I do that in Key Life's "Born Free" seminars.) However, there are some things you can do when you are intimidated by other people because of how you feel about yourself.

1. Recognize the truth about yourself. Check out those areas in the past where you have been shamed by your parents or others. Find an answer to the question: "Why do I always feel inferior, guilty, and afraid?" Look for traumatic events in your past that have shaped your present. Think about where you have failed and name those incidents. Bring out the secrets of the past that make you hesitant to talk and afraid to take risks. Shine the light on them and watch them die.

Anybody who has watched a horror film or read a horror book knows that demons die in the light. Most of our personal demons—past events that shape present reactions—will die in the light too. Frederick Buechner, in his book, *Telling Secrets,* talks about his father's suicide (the unspoken tragedy in his family) and his daughter's anorexia. Buechner makes a very profound statement in that book: "When we tell our secrets, even if only to ourself, they lose their power." (Harper & Row, 1991, p. 3)

Let me suggest that you find a trusted friend, your pastor, priest, or rabbi, or even a professional counselor, and reveal some secrets. Sometimes, the trauma of speaking is helped when you reveal to yourself and another person the source of that particular trauma.

2. Believe it or not, facing and doing that which we fear robs the fear of its power. There is an English saying that is quite helpful: "Fear knocked on the door; faith answered and nobody was there." In other words, if you have enough faith to go to the door, you will find that the awesome thing you feared has fled.

I remember the first time I ever spoke in public. I was in college and a little church in the mountains of North Carolina invited me to speak for their Sunday morning worship service. I had three pages of notes and, in my sermon practice, found that each page would take about eight minutes to deliver. But when the time came to give the sermon I had practiced, I went through the first page of my sermon in about two minutes. That, however, wasn't the worst part (a short speech is better than a long one anyway). The worst part was when I turned to the second page of my notes and found that page missing.

What did I do? Nothing. I just stood there and looked silly. Even as I tell you about the incident, I am blushing. It was a terrible morning. To be honest, my career as a public speaker almost came to an end that morning. All kinds of thoughts went through my mind. "I won't ever be this ashamed again because I will never do this again." I rationalized, "I am better at writing than I am at talking. So if someone asks me to speak again, I'll write the speech and let someone else give it." My career plans turned in a direction of vinyl repair.

But a friend cared enough about me to tell me what I'm going to tell you: The difference between a successful person and a failure is that the successful person got up the last time he or she was knocked down. My friend said that if I didn't speak again and do it soon, I would never do it again. And then he spoke an encouraging word, "Steve, hidden under your fear and your failure, there is a very rare gift. Don't bury it."

So I got up from being knocked down, and at the first opportunity (at a college meeting) I made another speech. Was I afraid? Of course I was afraid! Did I worry about it? Man, did I worry! But I'll tell you something else: I didn't lose my notes because I memorized the speech. I didn't make a great speech, but I didn't feel silly either.

What's the point? A good conversationalist or a good public speaker must risk—and continue to risk—until the demon dies. Roger Staubach, former quarterback for the Dallas Cowboys, was once asked how he felt when he had blown a pass. He said, "I can hardly wait to get my hands on the ball again." That's the reason he was a great quarterback.

It's okay to be afraid. It's even okay to feel intimidated. But it is not okay to quit. I'm not suggesting that you can eliminate your fear of others. I've never given a sermon, made a speech, or engaged in a conversation with someone who intimidated me that I wasn't afraid. That was okay. But it isn't okay to quit.

Marshall Ney, one of Napoleon's officers, would often say to his legs before going into battle: "Shake, will you! You would shake even more if you knew where I was going to take you today!" Just do it. Risk it. Stand up and, even if the fall is bad, get up over and over again. After a while (not quickly, but eventually), you will be able to think of what you are going to say more than how afraid you are to say it.

3. Learn to talk to yourself about who you are and what you feel. Imagine yourself doing well. Replace the negative tapes with positive ones.

I have some serious problems with the "guided imagery" of the New Age folks. First, it is silly, and second, it doesn't work. However, what I am saying here is quite different. The question before you is not whether you will paint pictures in your mind. We all imagine situations and how we will react in those situations. The only question is whether your imaginary picture of a situation will be positive or negative.

I know this seems somewhat like putting a Band-Aid on cancer, especially if one's background and self-image is horrible. However, you will be surprised at what can happen if you begin to see yourself as a scintillating conversationalist or a dynamic speaker (positive image) instead of a dull conversationalist and a bomb as a speaker (negative image).

Before playing golf, good golfers picture themselves hitting the ball with a proper swing and a long straight shot. Just so, a speaker ought to picture himself or herself speaking up in conversation, asking questions, giving opinions, presenting dazzling speeches, holding people's attention in giving a report. Learn to make positive tapes in your mind and play them over and over again. You will eventually become what you have imagined. It's called "fake it 'til you make it" and, believe it or not, it really works.

In other words, picture the role you want to play and then risk it. Eventually the role will become reality. I'm told that Dustin Hoffman, after playing his part as the autistic character in *Rain Man*, took months to begin to think in a normal fashion again. He had played the part so well that he became the part. Play the role of an actor and you will eventually find that the part becomes the reality.

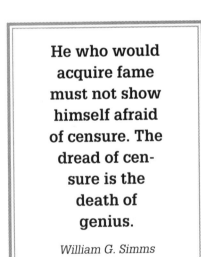

> **He who would acquire fame must not show himself afraid of censure. The dread of censure is the death of genius.**
>
> *William G. Simms*

Hostility Intimidates

Second, let's talk about the intimidating power of hostility.

You've heard that the best defense is a good offense. That is true because aggressiveness (often a manifestation of hostility) always catches people off guard and doesn't allow dialogue—only submission. Have you ever tried to talk to someone who was angry? That is always an unpleasant experience. If you are to continue to talk, most of your energy has to be invested in trying to calm the raging waters, not in sharing ideas or, in the case of a speech, in processing the ideas that are given. Hostility (whether in a speech or a conversation) does three things: eliminates communication, destroys goals, and creates more hostility.

There is one exception, however. Sometimes hostility is used as a technique of good communication. In that case it is *planned* hostility. It is the message of the angry prophet or the communication of an enemy intent, not on conversation, but on winning your submission. When hostility is planned, it can sometimes be effective in making a point, motivating an audience, or in winning an argument. But hostility, as a technique, is used only rarely by a good communicator and then in very measured doses.

I am the host of a live call-in radio program, and one of the interesting things about that kind of program is that a number of callers are hostile to me or to a position I have taken. I try to deal with those callers in what I hope is a creative way. After all, hostile calls are the "stuff" of a good talk show. However, each time I receive a hostile call, I find myself tensing up and becoming defensive.

That's true in conversation and in public speaking. When we know the recipient of our communication is hostile, we have a very difficult situation on our hands. Let me give you some simple ways to deal with the intimidation factor of hostility.

1. Remember that you are not required to talk to anyone. My job as a talk-show host, public speaker, and teacher does require that I sometimes confront hostile people. But, unless you are as weird as I am, *you* don't have to do that. When people react to you with hostility, try to remember that you are not a lamb being led to slaughter. Let me suggest that you say, "I don't have to listen to this. I like you, but until we can converse in a more subdued manner, I am going to do something else." And then walk away. My wife refuses to talk to me when I am angry. She knows that any kind of communication that takes place in the middle of my anger isn't going to be very productive. It's sort of like trying to teach a pig to sing. A pig doesn't sing very well anyway, and teaching him always makes him angry.

This is also true in speaking to audiences. I have a friend who was asked to speak for a required college chapel. For those of you who haven't been exposed to required chapel, let me explain. The students and faculty are required to be present at a particular chapel period. They miss it on pain of death. Not only that, attendance is always taken by noting who is or isn't in their seat. Speaking at required college chapels is my second least favorite thing in the world, the first being jumping off twenty-story buildings.

At any rate, my friend noticed that the students weren't listening and the professors were ignoring him (one was reading the paper). It was apparent to everyone, except the most dull, that there was "no way that dog was going to hunt."

This is how he opened and closed his speech: "It is apparent to me that you don't want to hear what I have to say any more than I want to say it. So, I'm history." With that he put his notes in his pocket and, to the astonishment of the audience, walked down the center aisle, out the auditorium door, got in his car, and drove off.

There is no rule that says that you have to engage in nonproductive conversation. There is no rule that says that you have to speak to a hostile audience. **2. Recognize that hostility is almost always a sign of insecurity.** When a person feels threatened enough to express anger, remember that it is a defense mechanism. A simple statement like, "A stuck pig usually squeals!" (or, if you would be a bit kinder, "I wonder why you are so angry. What it is that frightens you so?") will go a long way to dealing with the true cause of the anger and defusing it. Try to deal in a compassionate and gentle way, not only with the hostility, but also with the insecurity.

I was speaking to a group of students at the University of Miami about religion when, during the question-and-answer period, I noted a couple of very hostile students. Their questions were angry, and I had not said anything, I thought, that ought to have made them angry. And then, as I was listening to the fourth hostile question, I realized what was happening. Both students were Islamic. They had been dealing with the image of Islam in the American press that said, "Islam is made up of warmongers and fanatics." They had felt the harsh judgments of other students on the Islamic religion, and it went to the core of their worldview.

Once I understood that, I was able to deal with the real issue. I said, "You both are Islamic, aren't you?" They allowed they were. I then said, "Before I answer your question, let me say something important. I have been shocked at the way our American press has dealt with your religion. Our media is extremely superficial in their understanding of Christianity and Judaism, which are a part of our culture. But what they have done to your religion is criminal. If I were in your place, I would be highly offended." Then I answered the question.

The change in the attitude of those students was nothing less than amazing. As a matter of fact, after the meeting was over, they stayed around until the last person had left. One of the students said to me, "Dr. Brown, I just want to thank you for what you said. It is nice to see an American who does not agree with our religious views, but at the same time will treat us with respect."

Hostility that seems directed at you may not be aimed at you at all. I once stayed in a guest mission house in Africa. At the dinner table was a woman who was so hostile toward me (without reason, I might add) that I found myself reacting to her with hostility. I commented to someone that she reminded me of the "witch of Endor."

He said, "Steve, you have to excuse her. She has been on the mission field for over thirty years and next week she retires and goes back to the States. *This* has become her culture and her home, not the one she left in the United States. And yet, she must return and it is a very frightening and difficult time for her." Once I understood that, the dinner conversation the next evening was far more pleasant.

The point is this. Try to discover the source of the hostility and address—in your speech or your conversation—not the cognitive content of the anger, but its source.

3. Realize that sometimes it is necessary to greet hostility with hostility. Too often hostile people remain that way because they are never made to pay the price of their hostility. When we get to the chapter on how to win an argument, I'll have more to say about this, but for now let me say that anger sometimes needs to be confronted with anger. Sometimes, contrary to what your third-grade teacher told you, it is okay to be angry.

I once served as pastor of a church where a man had the reputation of "going after ministers." A number of people in the church warned me about him and his attitude. I called him into my study one day and said, "Sam, I understand that no pastor of this church has ever had to wonder what you were thinking. You, I understand, speak your mind."

"Well," he said uncomfortably, "I guess that's true."

"I just wanted you to know," I said, "that I think that is great. I give you permission to say to me whatever you want to say, to be angry and to correct me—as long as I have the same permission from you to say to you whatever I want to say, to be angry, and to correct you."

Over the years we fought a lot, but we both learned to deal with our anger far better than before because we had agreed to confront anger with anger. Too often angry people are ignored, borne with patience, or criticized behind their backs. The reason their anger only gets worse is that they have never had to pay the price for the anger. Sometimes it is well to say to an angry person, as I once did to a treasurer of an organization who started yelling at me: "You think you are angry. You don't know anything about anger. Right now you are looking at more restrained anger than you have ever seen in your lifetime." It was amazing how quickly he calmed down.

> **The secret of happiness is freedom, and the secret of freedom is courage.**
>
> *Gilbert Murray*

Position Intimidates

Now let's talk about the intimidating power of position.

Did you know that most Christians refuse to witness to anyone they consider to be on the higher rungs of a social ladder? We will talk about our faith to those we consider our inferiors and to those we consider our equals, but something happens when we are called to witness to someone we think is superior. That is a tragedy because it makes those who have reached the top of their profession, social class, or circle of friends quite lonely.

I have a friend who pastored a church in Cambridge, Massachusetts. At a party he met a prominent Harvard professor and the professor invited my friend to come and talk to him. An appointment was made, but when my friend showed up, the professor was late. My friend was ushered into the professor's office and told to wait. The professor would be there shortly.

As my friend looked at the book-lined office, the multitude of degrees and awards displayed on the wall, and as he thought about this professor's reputation he was, as you would have been, quite intimidated.

That was when my friend thought he heard from God.

"Tell the professor that Jesus loves him," my friend thought he heard.

"Lord, I can't do that. He is a brilliant scholar and I am a peon. He won't listen and will think I'm silly. I think I'll just sit here and ask questions. In the unlikely case that he says something I understand, I'll add a comment or two."

"Tell him that Jesus loves him," the message persisted.

Finally, my friend decided that he had been called to make a fool of himself. When the professor came in, my friend told him, as simply as he knew how, that Jesus loved him. That was when the professor broke down and cried.

We are all, to one degree or another, intimidated by position. Let me tell you some things that can help.

People who have achieved great prominence and position are usually more surprised than anybody that they achieved it. A study was done a number of years ago of presidents of large corporations. The researchers found that the most common fear among those leaders was that people would find out the truth about them—that a mistake had been made and they had been put in the wrong position.

I have spent a considerable part of my time talking to executives. Being a boy from the mountains of North Carolina, born on the wrong side of the tracks, I found myself being intimidated by those folks until Bill Bright told me that I had been called, among other things, to be involved with them.

You know something? The more I was with these "important people" the more I realized they were just as afraid as I was, just as lonely, just as guilty, and just as insecure—sometimes even more so. They had the ability to hide it better, but they were just like me. Once I understood that, the intimidation factor was no longer the problem it had been.

Often people in powerful positions are far more gracious and kind than you are given to believe by their portrayal in the media. The consummate villains in our society are the persons with position and prestige. They are portrayed as users, environmental monsters, and amoral twits. There are, of course, some people like that, but you would be surprised how quickly most respond with kindness to a kind remark, or with graciousness to a gracious person.

I had dinner with Arthur Burns a number of years ago. He had served a number of presidents and was considered by most people to be one of the finest minds in government and a genius in economics. At the beginning of the meal I said to him, "Dr. Burns, I can't balance my checkbook and I flunked math courses in college. So, if this dinner is going to be anything but a disaster for me, you are going to have to keep the fodder down low for this preacher."

He laughed. After that Burns was careful to address many of his remarks to me, to explain things I didn't understand, and to keep it simple. The best part of the whole dinner was that he never made me feel inferior or stupid.

Again, when speaking publicly to people of position and prestige or in a private conversation, one must be willing to take risks. Often people you believe had no felt needs for friendship, concern, and camaraderie are the most needy. The only way you can find out is to risk. If you risk, you may find a very pleasant surprise. You will find that underneath the protective facade is a real human being who will respond to you with far more warmth than you expected. (When someone doesn't respond that way, you will have learned something about twits.)

Expertise Intimidates

The fourth element in intimidation is the power of expertise.

There are some people who are so brilliant and gifted in their fields that you are intimidated because of their expertise.

I teach at a theological seminary, but you need to know that I ran away from kindergarten, and academic pursuits were a struggle thereafter. They call me "Doctor," but my doctorate is honorary, given to me by a college board in a moment of wild abandon. I am a full professor at the seminary because I "talk good" and they think I can teach theological students to communicate the good and heady stuff they have been learning. I suffer from no illusions about my brightness or my theological expertise.

Sometimes I speak in chapel at the seminary. You have no idea how intimidating that was until I realized that almost everything I said above about the intimidation of position and prestige also applies to the intimidation of expertise. Let me tell you some things that have helped me in this area.

My mother taught me that I was inferior to no other person and that I should not bow my head before anyone but

God. However, she was my mother and mothers are supposed to say things like that. So I continued to feel inferior until God told me the same thing my mother told me.

In the sixteenth century, when the poor scholar Muretus was found in the gutter and taken to the hospital, two physicians were discussing in Latin (so, they assumed, Muretus would not understand) whether or not to perform a new operation on him. One of the doctors asked, "Do you think we should do this surgery on this poor worthless creature?"

With that, Muretus raised himself from his hospital bed and said, "Wilt thou call that man worthless for whom Christ died?"

He was right. When I was a young pastor, my mentor told me that I should never leave the gravesite at a committal service before the family does. He said, "Steve, as they drive away, the family ought to see their pastor standing there at the grave of their departed loved one."

That was good advice, but the best part of it was what I learned by talking with the gravediggers after the family left. I remember one old cynical gravedigger on Cape Cod throwing in a shovelful of dirt. He turned, looked at me, took his cigar out of his mouth, and said, "You're a young one, ain't you?" Turning back to the grave, he said, "Reverend, that's all you get when you are dead: a hole and a shovelful of dirt."

Remember that whenever you talk to an expert, in far less than a hundred years, that person is going to be dead. Death is the great leveler of human beings and everybody stands equal before the grim reaper. Remembering that helps with the intimidation factor.

A second fact is that most experts aren't; or, if they are, they don't intimidate you with their expertise. We have treated doctors, theologians, some politicians, and attorneys like God for so long that some of them have come to believe it. That is dangerous to life and limb as well as to good conversation and public speaking.

I did my clinical training at a Boston hospital for the emotionally ill. The training consisted of spending considerable time on the wards with the patients, centering in on one or two patients and writing up "verbatims" on them.

I remember writing up my periodic encounters with one patient with whom I had become fairly close. In my report I offered some conclusions. I remember checking out the psychiatrist's records on this particular patient after I had written my own. I was shocked at how far I had missed the mark in my diagnosis.

I took my horribly flawed report to the professor and told him the mistake I had made. He said, "Steve, never assume that people, particularly psychiatrists, know more than they do know. I am familiar with this patient, and your report is more accurate than the psychiatrist's records. Learn to distrust the experts."

I remember how shocked I was. I had the same feeling when I was in the visitors' gallery of Congress and our leaders were debating the national budget. I always figured that they knew what they were doing. The most salient discovery of that visit was that these people were spending billions and billions of dollars of our money—and they didn't know any more than I knew. That was scary.

Always ask questions of your physicians and your attorneys until you understand what they are saying and can make your own judgment. Never assume that your pastor speaks from Sinai. Don't assume that because someone has written a book that he or she knows more than how to put a sentence together.

But, more important, don't be intimidated by experts. They are like you. That is not to say that one should not listen and assume expertise in an expert. After all, there will always be someone who knows more than you do about almost anything. That is what makes for good conversation and increases your knowledge. When you speak publicly to the experts, remember that you wouldn't be speaking if you didn't have something to say. So, say it without intimidation.

Circumstance Intimidates

Finally, there is the intimidating power of circumstance. This is when you find yourself in a circumstance you never sought, didn't ask for, and don't want, but nevertheless must face. Perhaps you are on a blind date or have inadvertently accepted a dinner invitation with people you don't know. Perhaps the audience you have been asked to address is quite different from what you were led to believe. Perhaps you find yourself overdressed (or underdressed) for a social occasion. It is the circumstance itself that does the intimidating.

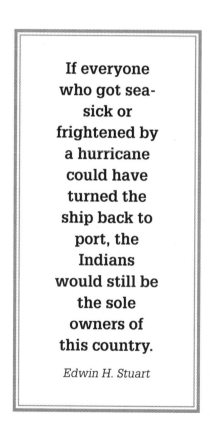

If everyone who got seasick or frightened by a hurricane could have turned the ship back to port, the Indians would still be the sole owners of this country.

Edwin H. Stuart

I was once asked to speak to a large ministry with a beach witnessing project in Hyannis on Cape Cod. It was my understanding that I was to speak to the staff members. When I got there, I found out that the staff had systematically combed the beach and the town streets looking for every drunk and reprobate they could find. They hustled them into an auditorium and introduced them to me with the expectation that I was going to say something meaningful to them.

Dear friend, it was the last place on the face of the earth where I wanted to be. I had not prepared to speak to that kind of audience and, even if I had, I don't know what I would have said to them. But there I was with the winos, the prostitutes, and the reprobates looking at me and waiting to see what I would say.

Would you believe that it was one of the truly great presentations in the history of Christendom? Well, would you believe that I did okay? As a matter of fact, I did. I even look back on the whole experience as rather exciting, and I learned some things that I have applied ever since.

Learn to tell the difference (as my friend, Fred Smith says) between problems and facts. A problem is something you can fix, and a fact is something you just have to accept. The serenity prayer reflects this understanding: "God, grant me the serenity to accept the things I cannot change, courage to change the things I can, and wisdom to know the difference."

Let me give you a related principle: "You can stand hell if you know you are going to get out." The corollary is this: "You always have the past to look forward to." So, accept a bad circumstance as something that you can't change, and make the best of it.

Some of the most pleasant experiences of life, God (or, if you're not a believer, "fate") disguises as an unpleasant circumstance. I remember one time finding myself at a dinner table with a group of radical feminists. I was speaking at the conference. Of all attendees, those women were the last ones with whom I wanted to have dinner. All the other chairs in the dining room had been taken. My alternatives were to go hungry or to make a fool of myself. So I sat down and tried to be as civil as possible.

Do you know what happened? It turned out to be an unusually gratifying experience. Surprisingly, their views were not what I expected and I enjoyed pursuing some subjects about which there had been some divisive and hurtful misunderstandings. Much to my astonishment, they wanted to know my opinions on a number of matters (under the rubric, I suspect, scientific study of an inferior species). It was a growing, and not an altogether unpleasant, experience.

Learn not to prejudge circumstances. Often there are great surprises awaiting those who are willing to make the best of what promised to be a terribly bad experience.

Jump, and let the devil take the hindmost. If circumstances are already bad, they probably won't get any worse. So you have nothing to lose. Some of the best conversations I have had and some of the best speeches I have made have taken place when I jumped into the circumstance with everything I had.

I am told that the female of a certain species of bird will start taking the nest apart when she can't get one of her children to fly. The mother knows that the small bird can fly, but the small bird doesn't know it. So, very slowly she starts taking the nest away, stick by stick, leaf by leaf.

I suspect that the small bird becomes quite disturbed with the bad circumstance. "MOTHER!!! What are you doing? Don't you care that I'm going to die? What kind of mother bird are you?"

And then, much to the surprise of the baby bird, he or she begins to flap those tiny wings and discovers the joy of flight. "Hey Mom!!! Look at me. I'm flying!"

God often puts us in circumstances where He wants to teach us to fly. He does that in life, and He also does that in teaching us to talk so people will listen. Go for it. If you don't, you will never know the truth about talking.

My friend Norm Evans told me once about a novice lineman on a college football team who went to his coach and said, "Coach, the opposing lineman keeps pulling my helmet down over my eyes. What should I do?"

The coach's answer was simple, direct, and classic: "Don't let him do it!"

If you are intimidated into silence by people and situations. . . don't let 'em do it.

3

Words with Authority

Naphtali is a deer let loose;
He uses beautiful words.
Gen. 49:21

At a cocktail party a woman and her husband approached a renowned physician. "Can you tell me," asked the wife, "why it is that some people are born mute?"

"Why," replied the doctor, "it is due either to a congenital inhibition of the faculty of articulation or to some anatomical deficiency in the organs of vocalization."

"There, see what it is to have an education?" the woman remarked, glaring triumphantly at her husband and then turning back to the doctor. "I've asked Henry that same question a hundred times. All he could say was, 'Because they're naturally born that way.'"

Of course, the point of the story is that someone who uses big words to describe a small truth can appear authoritative and wise. The truth may be just the opposite. Sometimes the best way to appear to be a jerk, is to use words that nobody understands. (And we will talk about that later.)

This chapter is about vocabulary and how to build it. In the introduction, I described speaking as a train that carries the product to the market. If I may continue with that metaphor, vocabulary constitutes the wheels on the train. The function of the wheels on a train is not that they are shiny or that they impress the folks who ride the train. The most important thing about those wheels is that they work.

If you want to talk so people will listen, it is essential that you have the right words for the message you want to communicate. This chapter on how to build a vocabulary will be, I should warn you, the dullest of the entire book. However, don't skip it. Often before you do something exciting, you must do a lot that is dull. ("Before you meet the charming prince, you have to kiss a lot of ugly frogs.") If you want to play the piano, build a bridge, or make a speech, there is always a prerequisite and the prerequisite is almost always monotonous and boring: practice, learn mathematical formulas, and learn vocabulary.

This is the plan. I want to show you the *wrong* way to build a vocabulary and then the *right* way.

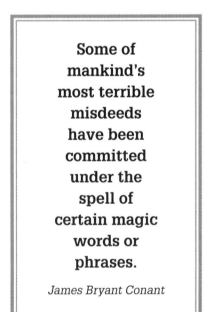

Some of mankind's most terrible misdeeds have been committed under the spell of certain magic words or phrases.

James Bryant Conant

Building a Vocabulary—the Wrong Way

Sometimes we learn more about how to do something by thinking about how not to do it.

(Edison, after finishing the five hundredth failure on a particular experiment was given some sympathy by a friend who said it was a shame to have lost so much time on unsuccessful experimentation. Edison said, "On the contrary. I now know five hundred ways not to do it.")

First, when building your vocabulary, don't memorize lists of words and their meanings. There is probably no method of building a vocabulary less effective than memorizing words. The problem with that methodology is that it is like buying a tool you will never use.

Jay Adams, in his helpful book, *Pulpit Speech* (Baker Book House, 1971), points out some studies showing that the average college student has a recognition vocabulary of about 250,000 words but uses only very few of them. Adams goes on to show that there are 20,000 common words but only 7,000 to 8,000 in everyday use. Milton used only slightly more than 11,000 different words and Shakespeare 25,000. (Have you ever wondered what kind of person would tabulate the words used by Milton or Shakespeare? I do hope our tax dollars didn't pay for the study.)

If you memorize words that have no relation to your daily use in speech, you will have a tendency to forget the words over a very short period of time. I have traveled to many of the countries of the world. Just before visiting a new country with a language different from English, I try to memorize a few basic phrases and sentences in the native language. ("I don't speak your language." "I'm hungry." "Good morning." "Good evening." "Where's the bathroom?") It's interesting that I don't remember any of those phrases or sentences now. Why? Because the foreign words I took the time to memorize are not words used in my daily speech. In other words, I memorized words that had no relation to the reality of my present life.

Words like *onomastic, Oogonium, zoogeography, penicilate* and *xenomorphic* may be fun to learn (if you are a word freak), but you won't remember them unless you use them. And if you do find yourself using them very often, you are even more weird than the person who memorizes them.

Second, from the listener's standpoint, when building a vocabulary, don't learn words that nobody else will understand. The purpose of speech is communication. Unless you are William Buckley (whose M.O. is the use of words nobody understands), the purpose of communication is first, to clearly communicate thoughts and second, to communicate those thoughts in ways that enhance and emphasize the thoughts.

There is one exception to this no-no about vocabulary. In a hostile, apathetic or polemical environment, one might sometimes want to use words, not to communicate, but to impress. I teach my students at the seminary that preachers have a major public relations problem in our society. Most preachers are viewed as silly, irrelevant, and superficial. I often tell the students that they should collect a few words in their homiletic bag that have no purpose other than to impress.

Black preaching is an art form that has the ability to motivate in ways that no other speaking style can. One of the finest practitioners of that art form is E. V. Hill. I have heard E. V. Hill on a number of occasions when he was addressing a primarily white audience. Dr. Hill will often, in his introduction, take off his glasses and "talk white." His technique is quite effective. He will speak in sophisticated, bland, and dull phrases, using words that would be used in a middle-class white pulpit. Then he will put his glasses on—the sign that he is going to preach. He is saying, "I just want to show you honkies that I can talk as bland as you can. Now that we have that straight, let's get down."

In the same way, a speaker may deliberately use words nobody understands (always, of course, in the proper context) simply to impress an audience or individual and thereby enhance receptivity for the message. But, on most occasions, long words spoken with authority will only lead to a horrible perception of the speaker. We live in a populist culture. (If you haven't noticed, you ought to pay attention.) Elitism, snobbishness, and pomposity are always the residual perception that flows from an overuse of words nobody understands.

One of my early mentors was Dr. John Stanton, a retired pastor in the Cape Cod village where I served my first church. Because he loved me and encouraged me, he had earned the right to say almost anything by way of criticism of my sermons. One Sunday at lunch he told me, "Steve, that was a wonderful sermon, but nobody understood it but you and me—and I wasn't sure." He then gave me a paperback version of *Roget's Thesaurus* and told me to use it. He said, "Whenever you have a nice sounding big word that might impress your professors at Boston University, use this little book to find a smaller one that will teach the same truth to your people in the church." I will be eternally grateful for his advice.

Third, when building a vocabulary, don't spend time learning words that are esoteric. Almost every profession or subculture has words used and understood by the members of that group and nobody else. The legal profession is notorious for using this kind of vocabulary, but some Christians, especially preachers, are even worse than lawyers.

Vance Havner, one of the most articulate and vital preachers America has ever produced has said this: "If you would try out a preacher, send him to preach to farmers; if he cannot make the grade there, let him reconsider his call." Good point. And it ought to be applied to a lot of folks who are given to using words understood only by a particular group. If you would try out a doctor, send him or her to talk to a teenager; if you would try out a lawyer, send him or her to talk to a construction worker; if you would try out an engineer, send him or her to talk to a philosopher; if you would try out a philosopher, send him or her to talk to a bartender. If he or she can't make it in those places, he or she ought to reconsider his or her calling.

Unless you are addressing someone, or an audience, in your subculture or your profession, make sure that the words you learn and use are universal words with universal meanings.

Building a Vocabulary—the Right Way

Now let me give you some ways to build the kind of vocabulary that can make a difference in communication.
Listen and read. Good communicators always listen to how others use words. They always read with a dictionary at hand and look up words they do not understand. One of the fortunate things about living in the twentieth century is that we are surrounded by powerful communicators. The down side of that is that to stand out from the crowd, you have to be a *very good* communicator. The up side of it is that there are so many models and sources from which one can not only learn good communication but also how words are used in good communication.

A good practice, especially if you have trouble with a limited vocabulary, is to make a goal of learning at least one or two words every

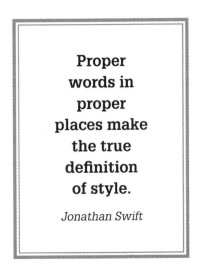

Proper words in proper places make the true definition of style.

Jonathan Swift

day. I hardly ever read a book, listen to a speech, talk with a friend, watch a television show, go to a movie, or pick up a newspaper that I don't learn a new word. All my life I have made it a practice to watch for new words that I could use in communication. A good practice is to keep a list of those words you have learned and periodically review the list.

Use the words that you have acquired. The rule is this: If you don't use it, you will lose it. That applies in a lot of areas and especially when building a vocabulary.

Suppose, for instance, that you read above the word *esoteric*, and it was a word with which you weren't familiar. Suppose, further, that you went to a dictionary and looked it up. If you did, you found that it means something understood by only a particular group of people and is pronounced "ess-uh-ter'-ik." Say it over and over again until you are familiar with its sound. Then put it in a sentence: "Doctors use such esoteric language that only a doctor can understand what another doctor is saying."

Look for places where you can use a new word. Use it often until you own it. Then it will be in the file system of your mind and you can always retrieve it when necessity arises.

Watch those times when you are grasping for the right word and find yourself using a weak substitute. We all do that, and the difference between a good communicator and a bad one is that the good one takes note of the incident and then makes sure that it doesn't happen again. "Full fluency" is how Jay Adams describes a necessary vocabulary. By that he means that a person who is talking should never have to search for the right word to describe the thought he or she is trying to communicate. When that happens to you, remember the incident and, at your first opportunity, find the word you should have used. You will

be surprised at how quickly your vocabulary will increase
by just "cleaning up the mess."

**Learn the difference between bland words and power
words.** George Walther's *Power Talking* (G. P. Putnam's
Sons, 1991) is a helpful book. I'm not talking here so much
about how to talk in ways that will give you power (we'll
say some things about that later) but about using words
that have emotional content.

For instance, "house" is bland while "home" has emotive power. "Stimulating" is bland while "exciting" or "sizzle" have power. When you use the word *fury* or *rage* for
anger, you will find that people will feel the power of the
word. Certain words solicit emotion: *America, mother, cow-
ardice, freedom, liberty, wrath, pervert.*

How do you learn the difference? By asking which
words "turn you on" and which words don't. Listen to
communicators who are able to move you with their
words. Make note of the words the communicator uses.
You will find over and over again that certain words have
power to move you. If they move you, there is a very good
chance that they will move others too. Learn to incorpo-
rate power words in your day-to-day conversation. (Be
careful, however, because the overuse of power words will
rob them of their power.)

**Expand your vocabulary to the point where you can
substitute a number of words for a particular word.** A
good game, especially when a speaker is dull, is to listen
to his or her words, and try to think of alternative words
that might have been used. That exercise will keep you
awake, and it will also increase your vocabulary.

I have a friend who is still one of the finest communicators I know. He is getting along in years. He told me that the
difficult thing about speaking publicly now was finding the
precise word to use in a speech. "But," he said, "my work
over the years in building a good vocabulary has really paid

> **The difference between the almost right word and the right word is really a large matter—'tis the difference between the lightning bug and the lightning.**
>
> *Mark Twain*

off. Every time one word won't come to mind, I think of five others."

A good communicator, one who talks so people will listen, will very rarely have trouble finding a word to match a thought. In fact, the real problem for a good communicator is deciding which of a number of possible words will communicate best the thought he or she desires to share.

I'm not big on rules, but let me give you a few that concern the use of words.

Using Words Successfully

1. Keep it simple. The goal of communication is not to impress but to communicate clearly. This is the origin of "It Floats," the Ivory soap slogan used a number of years ago. When the product was ready to market, a scientist, who had analyzed the elements of the soap, sent this memo: "The alkaline elements and vegetable fats in this product are blended in such a way as to secure the highest quality of saponification alone, with a specific gravity that keeps it on top of the water, relieving the bather of the trouble and annoyance of fishing around for it in the bottom during his ablutions." The advertising manager wrote in the margin of the memo: "It floats!" Those two words became the hallmark of the selling of Ivory soap.

We'll talk more about this in the next chapter, but for now it is well to remember that in a culture where "blah, blah, blah" is the mark of much that passes for conversation and speech, sometimes the most powerful talk is to say what you mean—simply, directly, and without fanfare. That is probably one of the things Jesus meant when he said that we ought to let our "yes" be "yes" and our "no" be "no." When was the last time you simply said "no" without elaboration or excuse? When was the last time you said "yes" without giving a million reasons why?

Arthur Mueller has a clever rewrite of the twenty-third Psalm: "The Lord is my external internal integrative mechanism. I shall not be deprived of gratifications for my vicerogenic hungers or my need-dispositions. He motivates me to orient myself towards a non-social object with effective significance. . . ." Try to evoke emotion with that. Paul Tillich, one of the great philosophical and theological thinkers of the last generation, was wont to call God, "The Ground of All Being." I suspect, if Tillich prayed that way, God would respond to his prayers with, "Say what?"

Work at using simple words, in clear-cut sentences that communicate focused ideas: "I like you." "I need a loan." "I want you to change your ways." "Will you do this for me?" "Be quiet!" "I don't think you know what you are talking about." "Go away!" Those are powerful sentences that communicate in very clear and succinct ways.

2. *Avoid using words that by overuse in inappropriate circumstances, have lost their original meaning.* Words like *fascist*, *racist*, and *fundamentalist* have lost any connection with their original meaning. They are useful words in building a verbal fire, but they have very little use in communicating a cognitive message. Words like *gentleman* (could mean anything from a wimp to a member of an audience), *saved* (saved what?), *love* (anything from a nice feeling to full-blown lust), or *Christian* (everything but Jews

and Moslems) simply are not precise enough to communicate a message.

3. Don't use curse words except in extreme circumstances. I believe that God has given us certain words with great power (curse words) that are to be used only on rare and special occasions. Believe it or not, the Bible contains some words that are softened when translated into English because of the tender ears of modern Christians. Martin Luther sometimes used language that would make a sailor blush. There are times when strong words of profanity seem appropriate. When you hit your finger with a hammer, "Mercy Teacups!" simply will not do.

The real problem with curse words often is that simple people with limited vocabularies, when looking for a proper word, revert to profanity as a line of least resistance.

Also, the more one uses a word, the more likely that word will lose its power. The modern media has destroyed some very good curse words with the constant bombardment of its audience with profanity. Each generation has its own curse words, and the words a culture defines as "unacceptable" change with each two or three generations. (For instance, earlier generations have defined curse words as *gosh* and *gee whiz*. Unless you have been living in the wilderness for a long, long time, you know that those words have about the power of a gnat crawling up a cow's tail with rape in mind.)

I would not want to be a scriptwriter for a modern movie in our culture. Words that had power have been used so often and so indiscriminately that there are few powerful words left. One almost has to dream up new kinds of profanity to do what "damn" would do a generation ago. Unless one is speaking to the most naive audience, a "damn" is no more powerful than a "darn." That is tragic for a communicator.

A further word on the use of profanity. Never, never use slang words that refer to bodily functions. It is simply in bad taste, and there are still people around who recognize and are offended by bad taste. When they see it in you, they will associate your vocabulary with your persona— and then they won't listen to *anything* you say. Few situations demand curse words. Only in the most extreme circumstances will a good communicator resort to that kind of language.

When in doubt, don't use any words. Silence sometimes communicates emotion more powerful than words.

A student once went to C. S. Lewis for a tutorial (an English practice where a professor and student work one on one). The student read his paper to Lewis and, during the reading of the paper, Lewis fell asleep. The student was furious and said that he had paid good money for his education and he expected comments on his work.

Lewis said, "Son, sleep *is* a comment."

4

Roadblocks to Communication

"... for it is not you who speak, but the Spirit of
your Father, who speaks in you."
Matt. 10:20

Did you hear about the man who was sitting on a tack?
Everyone was trying to help him deal with his pain. The
preachers told him it wouldn't hurt so much if he would
pray and study the Bible more. The sociologists said that
his pain was due to the social institutions that had molded
him. A psychologist said that the pain was intense because
his parents had potty trained him wrong. His wife said
that it was because he had not learned to be in touch with
his feelings.

Then a little boy walked by and asked, "Mister, why
don't you get off the tack?"

Remedying most communication problems, both one-
on-one and before a larger audience, can be as simple as
getting off the tack. This book is only one of thousands that
deal with how to talk so people will listen. However, most

problems with communication with other people happen, not because of a lack of information, but because of a glut of information. The solutions to those problems are far more simple than most folks think.

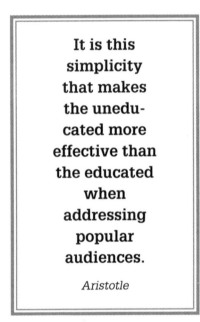

It is this simplicity that makes the unedu-cated more effective than the educated when addressing popular audiences.

Aristotle

I have watched videos on how to play golf. I have taken lessons and listened to the well-meaning advice of almost all of my friends on how to address the ball, the proper grip, stance, and swing. But the advice that helps me the most is the advice that is the most simple. It was given to me by the golf pro who said that my problem was too many helpful friends. He said, "Steve, keep your left arm straight and look at the ball. Forget about the rest." As long as I do that I play my best golf (which, at its best, leaves a lot to be desired). My problems magnify in direct proportion to how much I have to remember.

Most people make some basic mistakes or build "roadblocks to communication" when they talk. In this chapter I want to point them out to you. Don't let their simplicity fool you. Getting off a tack is simple too.

Temporizing the Message

The first roadblock to communication is not saying what we mean.

Most of us are so concerned with what people think of us and how we are saying things, that we fail to simply say what we mean. We are afraid that the one to whom we talk or the audience we address will be offended or hurt by our words, so we temporize the message. It isn't that we don't have the words, or that we don't know how to say them, or that we are confused. It's just that we are so supersensitive to others' feelings that we coat the message. Then the coating becomes the message.

Let me tell you a secret: Straightforward, unadorned, clear communication is so rare in our culture that when you hear it, its very simplicity is powerful.

Did you hear the story about the soldier whose mother had died? His sergeant didn't know how to tell him and felt quite uncomfortable in just "hitting him over the head" with the bad news. So the sergeant came up with what he thought was a compassionate and subtle way of telling the soldier about his mother's death. The next morning, when all

Sir Oswald Mosely, British Fascist leader, rose to speak at a rally of fascists. He raised his right arm in the fascist salute. The salute solicited cheers so the proud Mosely kept his arm raised. A heckler in the back of the auditorium shouted: "Yes, Oswald, you may go to the bathroom."

the troops were at attention for roll call, the sergeant said, "I want everyone who has a mother to take one step forward." And then he added, "Not so quick, George."

Over the years I have been the bearer of more bad news than I care to remember. I have told kids that a parent committed suicide. I have told families about the death of their children. Because I have relayed the news of disaster so often, I have become an expert. If the message is difficult, say it, say it simply and say it quickly.

That works with not only bad news, it applies to all communication. Simple messages—"I love you." "Would you have dinner with me?" "What you said made me angry!" "I don't want to do that because it makes me uncomfortable." "No" and "Yes" are powerful *because* they are simple.

Being Insensitive to Listeners

The second roadblock to communication comes when we take the first roadblock too far. We misunderstand how the person to whom we are communicating feels and thinks and thereby destroy good communication by insensitivity. In the next chapter, I'm going to say a lot about the importance of listening, but for now let me say that you need to know people if you want to talk to them. The best way to know a person is to listen.

We make a number of false assumptions about people that can get us into trouble when we try to communicate with them. For instance, we assume that they are just like us. This is particularly hazardous in communications between the genders. At the risk of sounding sexist, let me say that men and women are different. Don't assume that your spouse or friend thinks or feels or processes words the way you do. The man who watched the ambulance taking his wife away to the psychiatric ward who said, "I don't understand it, she never goes out of the kitchen," really didn't understand. "Of course I love her, I told her that when I married her. If I had changed my mind, I would have said so." That's the answer I received from a man I had asked about loving his wife.

Women do the same thing. A husband is more interested in what he is going to have for dinner than in how he feels about dinner. The reason he doesn't communicate what went on in the office is because he thinks you aren't interested. He probably believes he has a boring job anyway. Men dislike talking about abstract things, so if you ask a man how he is feeling about his love for you, he won't answer you because he never thought about it.

When I speak to a gathering of women, how I say something is quite different from how I would communicate the same message to a group of men. The packaging would be different. When I talk to men, it is important that I get them on my side before I say what needs to be said. This is particularly true of trying to talk to men about faith matters. When I talk to women, I don't have to do that. But I do have to be careful about the "feeling tone" of what I say. Women are far more sensitive to body language, tone of voice, and emotionally charged words than men are.

But the problem isn't just one between the sexes. It happens every day in formal and informal communication. It happens because there is simply no sensitivity to the other person's feelings. If I am speaking at a prison gathering, I can't say, "I'm glad you are all here." If I am talking to a teenager, I don't want to refer to Bach. If I am having a conversation with a homosexual, sexual proclivities need to be addressed very carefully, if at all. If I am talking to parents, I shouldn't criticize their kids. Of course, I could multiply the examples, and most of them (perhaps all of them) reflect simple common sense and sensitivity to other people.

Here's a principle that will help cut through all of the above: *There is a direct correlation between how much you value a person and the effectiveness of communication directed to that person.* If you listen closely and are reasonably caring, you won't make 90 percent of the communication errors of insensitivity.

One time Tolstoy was approached by a beggar who asked for money. Tolstoy replied, "Brother, I don't have any money, so I can't give you anything."

"But you have already given me a gift," replied the beggar. "You have called me 'brother,' and that is a great gift."

If I know that someone values me, I will probably understand what they are saying to me even if it isn't said well. Mark Twain's wife once got quite angry with him and began to curse. He started laughing and said, "My dear, you have the words right, but you don't know the tune." Well, the tune is placing value on the people to whom we talk. When that is right, even when the words are wrong, the message gets across. How often has someone said to another person in the context of love, "Oh, you know what I mean."

Sending Mixed Signals

The third roadblock to good communication is a failure to recognize that, as Roger Ailes says, you are the message. Charles Spurgeon, one of the greatest Christian communicators of the last two hundred years would often tell his students, "When you talk about heaven, let your facial expression reflect joy and

> **I speak Spanish to God, Italian to women, French to men and German to my horse.**
>
> *Emperor Charles V*

excitement. When you talk about hell, your normal expression will do." What he was saying is that communication involves far more than just words.

An editor of one of my books became a close friend over the months we worked together. After I had submitted the manuscript draft for the book (and his work was just beginning), he called me and asked, "Steve, is this the way you really talk?" I allowed that it was and he said, "That's all I wanted to know." He edited the manuscript with the knowledge that *I* was as much a part of the message as the message itself.

If a person doesn't like you, it stands to reason that he or she won't like what you say. If you are not enthusiastic about your message, no one else is going to be enthusiastic about it either. If you don't speak with authority, most folks will assume that you don't know what you are talking about. If you come across as an adversary in your communication style (and sometimes you want to), you need to know that the response you get will be adversarial. If you have "shifty eyes" and refuse to look at the people to whom you communicate, they are going to think you are lying.

The point is this: What you are, how you talk, and the way you look make up the "stuff" of communication. If you overlook that, you will find that communication simply will not take place.

One of the real problems I have is that my voice doesn't fit the way I look. For some reason, God has given me a very deep voice. I sound like the Marlboro Man, but I look like a rather large and sinister Mr. Peepers. (Someone once suggested that I have the perfect radio face.) When I speak at rallies, conferences, or seminars, the people in attendance who have listened to my radio program almost always initially express shock. When I meet people individually, they sometimes say, "No, you're not Steve Brown."

I often say, "Yes, I am. I got a letter this morning and it was addressed to Steve Brown."

Listen up! I'm going to give you a living illustration of this point. Please note that I have dealt with the problem of my looks and my voice by trying to be humorous. When dealing with an audience or an individual who is plainly disturbed by the conflict between the way I look and the way I sound, I have a number of options. I could, for instance, act offended and say something like, "I think you are quite insensitive to my feelings, and I may cry." Or I could wear shoes that have elevator soles and heels, padded shirts, and a black leather motorcycle jacket with a skull and crossbones on the back. I would thereby look a little more like I sound. Or I could just ignore the obvious shock. But those methodologies are not helpful in doing what I do for a living, communicating a particular message.

What I've discovered is that I can enhance my message by not taking myself too seriously. By treating the whole subject of the dichotomy between my looks and my voice with humor, I have opened wide the possibility of good communication. I have learned, at least in this area, that *I* am the message.

Learn to pay attention to something besides the words you use. Ask some trusted friends about how you come across to other people. Don't speak to a formal gathering in a bathing suit, and don't do beach evangelism in a suit and tie (especially if you are a woman) or a formal dress (especially if you are a man). Don't giggle at funerals and don't burp at weddings because you are the message.

Disregarding Responses

The fourth roadblock to good communication is being so concerned with yourself that you don't pay attention to

> **A word is dead**
>
> **When it is said,**
>
> **Some say.**
>
> **I say it just**
>
> **Begins to live**
>
> **That day.**
>
> *Emily Dickinson, 1872*

what is being said by the other person.

In marriage counseling, when it becomes clear that the two parties aren't communicating, I will often suggest a game. I tell the couple, "We are going to play Communication. Here are the rules. I want each of you to address your feelings and your thoughts to the other, but the other person must respond by telling you what you just said and then you must agree that it is what you said."

I often will tell the wife to go first, and she is usually happy to take that position. For once, she figures, she has a referee. So she begins to blast away.

Her husband will usually interrupt and I'll have to say, "Just be quiet. You will get your chance." So he stays quiet until she finishes. And then he blasts off. I will say, "Wait just a minute. You have to tell her exactly what she just said before you get your chance."

"I know what she said," he will respond.

"Well, tell her."

"Okay," he will say with great resignation. "This is what you said." Then he will proceed to tell his wife what he thinks she just said.

"That's not what I said at all," she will say.

"Well," I say, "tell him again."

So she goes at him again. I often notice that he is listening a bit more intently this time because he knows that if he doesn't get it right, he is never going to be able to say his piece. When it is his turn, finally, to speak, the whole thing starts all over again. There have been times when both husband and wife have had to repeat their message as many as three or four times before the other got it right.

A good practice in communication is to say to the other person, "Let me see if I have it right. As I heard you, this is what you said." Your response is often far better when you have understood what was going on in the conversation.

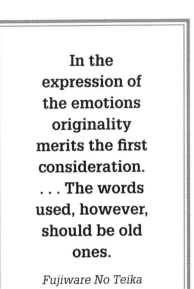

In the expression of the emotions originality merits the first consideration. . . . The words used, however, should be old ones.

Fujiware No Teika

Failing to Define Terms

The final roadblock to good communication is a failure to define terms. In a good debate, the first step is to define terms. Otherwise, a debate can degenerate into a shouting match with no substance.

Those of us who are Christians have a special problem in this area. When I was a pastor, the denomination (and my personal convictions) required that I should not perform a marriage ceremony for a Christian and a non-Christian. Marriage is difficult enough without a disagreement over something as important as religion. If there is no agreement there, then the odds of marriage failure go through the roof. So, as a matter of principle and practical concern, I simply did not perform the wedding ceremony for believers and nonbelievers. In other words, I refused to cross-fertilize.

One of the problems with the term *Christian* is that it has been so overused in our culture that it almost doesn't mean anything anymore. A Christian, most folks believe, is anybody who is not a Jew. So, I found it necessary in my premarital counseling to say, "Look, I have a rule that is important to me and certainly not a judgment on you. I can't marry a Christian to a non-Christian. But before you jump to a hasty conclusion, let me explain what I mean by *Christian*. It doesn't mean that you go to church on Easter or even that you are a church member. [If you sleep in a garage, it doesn't make you a car.] By 'Christian,' I mean someone who has a personal commitment to Jesus Christ and accepts the forgiveness of God on the basis of Christ's sacrifice."

I have found that when I so define the term, I get understanding. Then there isn't confusion about the message I'm trying to communicate. And, surprisingly, I find that people are not angry at the message I'm communicating. Often I have had engaged couples say to me, "Reverend, I now understand what you mean, and we don't fit that definition. I guess we should ask someone else to perform the ceremony."

Someone once said to an atheist, "Tell me the kind of God you don't believe in. I probably don't believe in that kind of God either." What do you mean by the word *God*? What do you mean by *any* word you use? Once that is settled, then you and your audience will be talking about the same thing.

Those are the roadblocks. They are simple, but they are true. Learn them and you're most of the way home.

5

No Wasted Conversation

Let no corrupt communication proceed out
of your mouth, but what is good for
necessary edification, that it may impart
grace to the hearers.
Eph. 4:29

Before we turn to the subject at hand—how to be a good conversationalist—let me give you a word of caution: The principles I am going to give you in this chapter can become quite manipulative if misused. In other words, I'm going to show you how to motivate people through conversation. But anything used to motivate can also be used to manipulate. The difference between "motivation" and "manipulation" is that manipulation is for *my* benefit and motivation is for *their* (or *our*) benefit.

These principles are amoral. It is not the automobile that kills; it is the drunk driving the automobile. Just so, with principles of good conversation, you could achieve personal power over others, accomplish your selfish goals, and enhance your own interests. However, that is not my intent.

I'm not your mother and certainly am not responsible for what you do with the message of this chapter or the message of this book, but let me tell you something you ought to remember: People who are manipulative almost always end up lonely, paranoid, and often do not achieve the goals they desire. You see, there are laws built into the universe (believers know that God put them there) that will destroy those who violate them.

A number of years ago, my friend Marabel Morgan wrote a book titled *The Total Woman*. The book sold hundreds of thousands of copies, and Marabel became a celebrity almost overnight. She appeared on television and radio talk shows across the nation and was featured in almost every major magazine and newspaper in the country. Her face was on the cover of *Time* magazine and a number of other prominent publications.

During those years, I was Marabel's pastor. She often asked me to help answer some of the thousands of letters she received. Those letters were mostly from women (no surprise), and the women were of two types. One group selfishly wanted to get their husbands to be what they wanted them to be. Their letters asked questions about how to "manipulate" a husband by using the principles taught in Marabel's book.

However, the other group consisted of women who loved their husbands and wanted to know better how to please them. Their motivation was love, and they saw Marabel's principles as a way to understand and please their husbands. Wanting to please a husband or a wife one loves is a natural desire.

Marabel was constantly being challenged by accusations that her book was manipulative. She always answered those charges (and, by the way, is living out her answers in her own life and marriage) by saying, "I love my husband, and I have discovered ways to please him. I want to give him pleasure because I love him—not because I want to manipulate him."

One thing that I noticed about those who applied the principles Marabel taught in her book was that if the one who applied the principles was trying to manipulate, after an initial burst of success with the marriage, the marriage ended up worse than before. However, in those cases where Marabel's book became a handbook showing women how to love their husbands better, the results were astounding.

It is the same way with the principles I teach in this book. If your object is to gain power through manipulation, then—like the proverbial rubber band stretched too far—it is going to snap back and get you. But if you want to be a better communicator because you are others-directed and want to display your ideas in the best possible light, these principles are going to create a better life for you.

Enough of that. Let's get on with the basic principles of good conversation. There are three of them and also a number of implications which either directly or

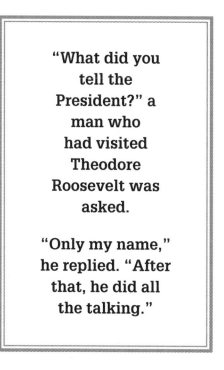

"What did you tell the President?" a man who had visited Theodore Roosevelt was asked.

"Only my name," he replied. "After that, he did all the talking."

indirectly follow them. In the last part of this chapter I want to apply the principles and their applications in some practical ways.

Conversation: Rule 1

The first principle is a principle of life as well as a principle of communication. Once you understand it, it will enable you not only to master the basics of good conversation, but also to master some basics of good relationships. This is the principle: *Generally, people are more interested in themselves than they are in you.* The corollary is that you are basically more interested in yourself than you are in other people.

A friend of mine once asked me, "Steve, do you ever wonder what people are thinking about you?" When I allowed that I wouldn't mind having that kind of information, he laughed and said, "They aren't thinking about you at all!"

He was right! Not only was he right, but the fact that I was concerned about what people were thinking about me is confirmation that, generally, I am more interested in myself than in other people. And the fact that people are *not* thinking about me is confirmation of the fact that people are generally more interested in themselves than in others.

Now, with that as a basic principle of communication, let's draw some implications that will aid you in conversation. There are five.

Implications of Rule 1

1. An others-directed person will always be seen as a good conversationalist. Did you hear about the famous, egotistic author who said to his friend, "We have only been talking about me. Let's talk about you. What did you think of my latest book?"

Too many of us are like that author. Nothing is of real interest unless it concerns me and my concerns. If you are interested only in talking about your concerns, and the person to whom you are speaking is only interested in talking about his or her own concerns, it doesn't take a brain surgeon to understand that not much is going to happen by way of conversation.

If you have the ability to subordinate your interests to those of another person, you have already understood 80 percent of what it takes to be considered by your friends and acquaintances as a wonderful conversationalist.

2. In a good conversation, listening is as important as talking. Have you ever had a conversation with someone who seemed to only be waiting until you finished for him or her to talk? Have you ever received responses from people that showed they didn't have the faintest idea of what you just said? Have you ever noticed the "wandering eyes" of someone to whom you were talking and then realized that the person was apparently using you until someone more interesting came along? Have you ever said something you thought was important to someone and then, in their response, realized that what was important to you was not important to them? It was almost as if the person had said, "Here's a quarter. Call someone who cares." Do you remember how you felt when that happened? Although nothing was said, it was clear that the listener thought you were ugly and that your mother dressed you funny.

If you didn't like it, there is a good chance that others won't like it either.

3. Responding without condemnation or judgment will keep a good conversation going. Conversely, responding with condemnation or judgment will bring a good conversation to an abrupt end. Some people simply are unable to say anything positive about or to anyone else. In every conversation someone gets "roasted."

Some people make me feel guilty when I'm within ten yards of them. They are always looking down long noses in my direction. Almost always, around that kind of person, I find that I don't want to say anything, for fear of being criticized. I don't want to offer an opinion (it will be wrong), ask a question (it will always be a dumb one), or make a comment (it will be the subject of silent derision).

My mentor Fred Smith often says that a wise man or woman is someone who knows that there is no sin of which he or she is not capable. I took Fred's comment to heart and, as a result, over the last twenty years have had a very busy counseling ministry. Hundreds of people have come to me for help, and sometimes (I hope more often than not) I have been able to say some reasonably intelligent and helpful things to them. But that isn't the reason so many people came. It had nothing to do with my wisdom or my insights. They came mainly because I accepted them without judgment or condemnation.

I would often say to someone who had come to me for help, "Look, I've been doing this for a lot of years. You need to know right off that you aren't going to tell me anything that I haven't heard before. You will find it is impossible to shock me, and I don't ever talk to anyone about anything you say to me. I don't even talk in my sleep. But, more important than that, there is nothing you can say that will cause me to think less of you. I like you just because you are you."

Clergymen are often seen as rather critical and judgmental people, so some of the people who heard my little speech were not a little surprised. But more important than that, because they were accepted, they often poured out their hearts to me. Over and over again, people would say,

"Steve, I've never told anyone this before but. . . ." I considered it a high and holy privilege to be allowed to share their secrets, to cry when they were in pain, and to rejoice with them in their successes.

I learned that from Jesus, who treats us all that way. (It's hard to accept others until you have been accepted—and then you can accept others only to the degree to which you have been accepted. Because I know Jesus had accepted me, I was able to accept others.) The reason Jesus was always surrounded by winos and prostitutes was because he talked with them and laughed with them without condemnation. Whether or not you are a believer, the example of Jesus provides a model of what makes a good conversation happen.

One other thing about conversation before we leave this point: Not only should our conversation be accepting and nonjudgmental toward the one to whom we are talking, we also need to be careful about saying negative things regarding absent third parties. I'm not suggesting that good conversation is always positive. What I am saying is that negative people don't attract other negative people— they don't attract anyone. A bit of good-natured gossip can add spice to any conversation. (For instance, there are some politicians about whom one can say very little that is positive.) If conversation is never about people, it very shortly becomes dull conversation. There is only so much you can say about the weather, but when conversation degenerates to a roasting session of other people, it becomes a turnoff.

4. Conversation, especially with a new acquaintance, will move more smoothly when you converse within the parameters of the other person's interests. This, of course, is another way to say some of what I've said above, but there is a different twist to it. When I meet someone for the first time, I make an effort to find out about that person's family, about what that person does for a living, about where they live, and about their general interests. If I'm talking to a preacher, I don't have to ask. I know what preachers like. Similarly, when I talk to a parent or an athlete or a politician, without asking I can ascertain the interest area of the person to whom I'm talking. For others, it is a bit more difficult, but always easily done if one is willing to ask questions and to listen.

5. *When you think you are bungling a conversation, there is a very good chance that the other person won't even notice.* Because people are generally more interested in themselves than in you and what you say, most people are not as shocked, as upset, or even as aware of your *faux pas* as you are.

I have found that one reason most people don't consider themselves good conversationalists is that they feel they are always saying something "stupid." Let me tell you a wonderful secret that all good conversationalists know: Others won't even notice. Time after time I have had people say to me, "Steve, when we talked, I hope you didn't think what I said was too silly. I couldn't believe I would say something that stupid." On such occasions, I usually couldn't remember what it was that they said.

You see, I was so busy being interested in me and my concerns that I didn't have time to notice the other person's silly statements. Most people are that way. Remember that the next time you blush because of something you said.

> **When you talk, you only say something that you already know. When you listen, you learn what someone else knows.**
>
> *Anonymous*

Conversation: Rule 2

The second principle of good conversation is this: *The parameters of a conversation should be set by the nature of your relationship to the one with whom you are speaking.* In other words, you have to earn the right to have more than a superficial conversation. There are some implications of this principle too.

Implications of Rule 2

1. The "comfort zone" within a conversation should never be violated. The comfort zone of people with whom you talk will vary and expand depending on the nature of the relationship you have. Conversations deepen in terms of feelings and honesty in direct proportion to the depth of the relationship.

During my daily radio broadcasts I will sometimes say on the air, "I very much appreciate the fact that you invite me into your home each day. I consider it a high and holy privilege." On one occasion, in what was probably a poor attempt at humor, I went on to say, "But, to be perfectly honest with you, your housekeeping leaves something to be desired."

This is a response I received:

Dear Steve,

My feelings were deeply hurt by one of your "jokes," and that diminished my enthusiasm for your program. Your comment about my poor housekeeping right on the heels of thanking me for welcoming you as a trusted guest in my home hit a very sore place in my heart. You know of my social isolation and loneliness. Were you taking a "cheap shot" at me?

What happened? I had violated this woman's comfort zone. I, of course, was not taking a "cheap shot" at her housekeeping. We receive thousands of letters each month at our offices. If she had told me about her difficulty in this area, I certainly did not see the letter. However, because that was an area where she was quite uncomfortable, what I said went to the heart of her place of embarrassment. While that was excusable on a broadcast, it would be inexcusable in a one-on-one conversation.

One does not talk about sex to the town prude. Someone to the right of Genghis Khan does not express political views to a liberal who is just this side of "the sky is the limit." One does not (on a more serious level) in an initial conversation assume the total freedom that only time and relationship will establish. Start with the weather, sports, and the movies before you discuss more serious issues. A good conversationalist knows that one must earn the right to discuss some issues.

2. Beginning conversation is better conducted with facts rather than with feelings. Someone (probably a "sexist pig") has said that men talk about events and things and women talk about feelings. There is probably some truth in that. If you are wondering what your husband's deepest feelings are, it may be that he is just hungry. I have noticed that women seem more "in touch" (don't you hate that phrase?) with their emotions in the sense that—without a lot of effort—a woman can often tell you exactly what she *feels* and why.

Aside from the gender differences, when talking with a new friend, it is always wise to keep the conversation centered around facts. Most people find those kinds of subjects less threatening than conversations about feelings. As a relationship deepens, one can then expand the parameters of conversation.

> **The great gift of conversation lies less in displaying it ourselves than in drawing it out of others. He who leaves your company pleased with himself and his own cleverness is perfectly well pleased with you.**
>
> *Jean de La Bruyère*

Conversation: Rule 3

The third and final principle of good conversation is this: *Conversation is always harder to start than it is to continue.* Two implications follow.

Implications of Rule 3

1. Almost all planning about the direction of conversation is wasted effort. One ought to plan how to start a conversation but not how to keep it going. Later in this chapter I'll suggest some good and practical "conversation starters." Some of you are going to want more than a starter. You want to know what to say after a conversation gets going. Trust me on this: You don't need more than a starter. Like the engine of a car, once conversation gets going, it can be maintained with little effort or planning.

When I worked in commercial broadcasting, pianist Roger Williams was giving a concert in the city where I did an evening radio show. The program director wanted someone to interview Williams. Even though I was the youngest man on the staff and had never done an interview in my life, I was the only one at the station available, so I was sent.

I remember walking into the auditorium where Roger Williams was sitting at the piano practicing scales. As I listened to him, I decided that the best plan of action would be to "fake it until I made it." I planned to walk up and say, "Mr. Williams, I'm from WGBG and, as the top interviewer in this city, was sent to conduct an interview with you." But the more I thought about it, the more I realized there was no way I was going to be able to pull that off.

When I walked up to the piano, Roger Williams stopped playing and turned to me. I said, "Mr. Williams, I'm from WGBG, and I'm supposed to interview you. I would like to tell you that I'm really good at this, but that would be a lie. The only reason they sent me was because I was the only one available. So, if you want to do this interview, I would like to do it. But, if you would prefer to wait for someone more versed in this art, my feelings wouldn't be hurt."

Williams laughed, walked to the back of the stage, and pulled a chair up to the piano. "Son," he said, "sit down here. I appreciate your honesty. Let me give you the first question to ask. Make sure you listen to my answer and you will know what question to ask next from how I answered the first question. We will continue through the interview that way. All you have to do is to listen carefully and do what comes naturally."

It was a great interview! (In fact, I think it was one of the great interviews in the history of American broadcasting.) When I got back to the station, my program director said, "Steve, that's fantastic! I didn't know you had it in you." I responded with something like, "I guess some people are naturally good at this business." At the station, I received a new degree of respect.

What's the point? What Roger Williams taught me in that interview is true in all conversation. Don't worry so much about what you are going to say or how you are going to respond. Just listen very carefully, and then do (conversationally, of course) what comes naturally.

2. "Going with the flow" in conversation is far better than bringing an agenda to the conversation. Because of the books I write, I am often interviewed by Christian broadcasters on stations around the country. Whenever the interviewer brings to the interview the list of questions prepared by the publisher, I know I'm in trouble. But those interviewers who don't know who I am and have never read my books, but who have a consuming interest in me and what I have written will always shine in an interview.

It is the same way with conversation, as opposed to public speaking, giving a report, or making a sale. Conversation occurs when two people share something of themselves with each other. Conversation is stifled when you or I bring agendas to the conversation. People are interesting, every person has a story and, without exception, people bring to conversational encounters a worthwhile and valuable contribution. Learn to develop an interest in "going with the flow" of the conversation by setting aside your agenda. You will be surprised the diamonds that will be mined thereby.

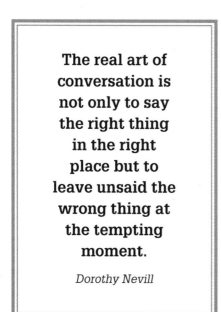

> The real art of conversation is not only to say the right thing in the right place but to leave unsaid the wrong thing at the tempting moment.
>
> Dorothy Nevill

Practical Helps

Now let's take these principles and move to some practical help in becoming a good conversationalist. A conversation has a commencement, a core, and a close (the three "C's"). Let's take each of those elements and examine them in some detail.

1. The Commencement. As mentioned above, this is the most important part of the conversation. At the beginning it is important that you focus on the other person. Incidentally, the reason most of us don't remember names is that we are focused on ourselves and the impression we are making.

In an initial conversation, always open by giving your name, even if you think the other person ought to know your name. Never assume that someone knows your name. They may be as self-oriented as you are. Begin with, "Hi, I'm Sara Smith . . ." to be followed with a non-threatening conversation starter. Let me give you a very short list of good conversation starters. Think about it, and you can add to the list.

"I noticed that dress you were wearing. Where did you get it? I really like it."

"You were standing by yourself, so I thought I would come over and meet you. I'm. . . ."

"I thought that was a good report [sermon, program, movie, etc.]. What did you think?"

"Man, this heat [cold, wind, humidity, etc.] is getting to me. You don't seem to let it bother you. How do you do it?"

"I saw you at the meeting [church, club, park, etc.] this afternoon and said to myself, 'Myself, I would really like to get to know him/her.' My name is Jack Smith. How did you feel the meeting went?"

"How about them Yankees?"

Enough of that. You get the idea.

2. The Core. This is the easiest part of the conversation. If you are sensitive to the flow of a conversation, you will find no trouble in maintaining that flow. We are social beings, and when we give reign to those social impulses instead of bottling them up with fear, self-centeredness or manipulation, a conversation takes its natural flow.

In the core of the conversation, don't be afraid of pauses or periods of silences. Those pauses may indicate the cessation of the conversation or they may be just a pause where the participants regroup and think.

I talk for a living. The danger of talking for a living is that one has a tendency to be very uncomfortable with silence. Whenever there is a pause, I feel constrained to fill it. It doesn't matter what I say or if I have anything meaningful to say—I just keep talking until something comes to mind. A friend of mine who loved me enough to tell me the truth said, "Steve, you don't have to be filler in a conversation. Silence is sometimes the best part of a conversation."

I have already placed a heavy emphasis on listening and asking questions. I have said that a good conversationalist must be others-directed. However, it is also well to remember that a conversation is an encounter between two people. It is therefore important that each one pulls a share of the conversational load. Offer your opinions and observations too. It is important that each one not only be a good listener but also be a good responder.

If you don't know something about the subject being discussed, don't pretend. Say you don't know or understand and then ask questions. The other people in the conversation will, rather than being affected by your ignorance, be impressed with their own brilliance. However, when you have something to add . . . add it.

3. The Closing. In psychological counseling, the most difficult period for therapist and client is that time that is referred to as "termination." That is true of conversation too. Termination can, if handled improperly, seem to be a judgment on another person—like saying, "I just don't want to talk to you anymore." That is why it is important that the close of a conversation be definite and always be done with a legitimate reason. Some examples:

"Man, I've got to go. I didn't realize we had talked so long."

"It's been really great talking to you. I hope we can get together again. I've enjoyed this, but if I don't get home my wife [husband] is going to ask for a divorce."

"I've got an appointment, so I've got to get out of here. I'll look forward to the next time we have a chance to talk."

By giving it a little thought and practice, you can build your own list of conversation terminators. The rule is to make sure that when you end the conversation, the person with whom you are talking doesn't wonder whether you think he or she has bad breath. Of course, there are times when you want to communicate a desire never to talk to a certain person again. In that case, skip the Binaca.

Overcoming Hindrances

One more area I want to cover before we move on is some of the general problems people encounter in conversation.

How to deal with anxiety. One of the hindrances to good conversation is anxiety about one's ability to be able to carry on a good conversation. We are often afraid of saying something stupid, so we don't say anything. If

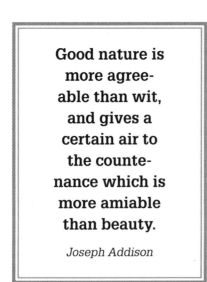

Good nature is more agreeable than wit, and gives a certain air to the countenance which is more amiable than beauty.

Joseph Addison

people intimidate us, we avoid extended conversations. Insecurity blocks our ability to be a good responder in a conversation.

Listen up! I'm going to give you a secret that every successful conversationalist knows but hasn't told you. Everybody is insecure; everybody is anxious about making a good impression; everybody is afraid of saying the wrong thing. Just remember that, and don't tell anybody the secret. It will increase your comfort zone considerably.

Learn to ask yourself this question: "If I weren't intimidated—if I weren't so insecure and filled with anxiety—how would I act? What would I say and what would I do?" Then act. Say it. You will be surprised at how quickly the "act" will become a reality.

How to deal with rejection. I am quite sensitive. You are too. Those who tell you that they aren't sensitive, that they don't mind criticism, or that rejection is easy, will lie about other things. We all want people to think well of us. We all want to be admired, listened to, and respected. There are four basic adult fears: rejection, failure, punishment, and shame. Please note that all four have to do with others' reactions to us.

Learn not to evaluate yourself by rejection. You are valuable, you are acceptable, and you are important, no matter how twits react to you. (Of course, if everybody rejects you, you might want to get some help.) I receive thousands of letters each month as a result of our radio broadcast. Do you know the hardest thing about reading those letters? Ten percent of them are critical. I've learned to look at the 90 percent without ignoring the 10 percent. You probably run about the same percentage in the reactions you receive from others.

Jesus said that we ought to beware of that time when all people speak well of us. He didn't explain further, but I suspect the reason he said it was that if everybody likes you and admires you, you are probably very dull or very dead.

Learn the art of affirming people, and learn to develop relationships with others who have developed that art. We can all start with our mothers, but we can expand it to a whole lot of other people. Evaluate criticism and rejection but don't assume that the criticism is always justified or that the rejection is proper. Consider the source. The criticism may come from a Bozo and the rejection may come from someone who just recently gave you a compliment.

A certain young man, after visiting the National Gallery of Art in Washington, told the guard that he didn't much like the paintings. The guard replied, "Son, these paintings aren't on trial. You are."

How to deal with a twit. Honesty is always the best policy in dealing with some people. There are those negative, critical or angry souls who simply will not go away. The reason most of us don't deal with those kinds of people is that we are afraid of what they will think of us. Just remember that your mother loves you and say, "Sam [or Gertrude], I really have a problem with our relationship and I'm not going to be able to continue it. The problem may be mine, but I can't be your friend anymore because. . ." (and then name the reason). That kind of honesty may scare you to death at first, but it will become addictive and you won't feel so "dirty" about your dishonesty.

How to deal with accurate criticism. Sometimes criticism comes from one who has a critical spirit, but there are other times when someone loves us enough to tell us the truth. I have a priest friend in Miami who carries a card with him. On one side it says, "Bless those who curse you. . . ." On the other side it says, ". . . they may be right."

I have a group of friends I have learned to trust. (I would recommend this practice.) They will always be honest with me. I have learned to take criticism I have received from one or more of those friends. I will say, "Eddie, let me tell you something that came up in conversation this afternoon. I need to check it with you to see if you think what was said about me is accurate." I can depend on my friend to (albeit, gently) tell me the truth. If you don't have friends like that, develop some. They are more valuable than knowing algebra.

A final important word. *Develop a little bit of humility—please.* Someone said, in response to a man who bragged that he was "self-made," "That is good. It relieves the Lord of a great responsibility." Human beings are a mix of good and bad, success and failure, wit and stupidity, love and hate, and being right and wrong. Nobody in a conversation, or in any other situation, can speak as an outsider of the human race.

You have a right to be human. That means that you have a right to fail sometimes, to be wrong sometimes, and to do and say stupid things sometimes. Don't try to cover it. When you do, you remove yourself from the human race. Know-it-alls make poor conversationalists and worse friends. Learn to laugh at yourself, and others will laugh *with* you. Don't laugh at yourself and others will laugh at you—behind your back.

The best conversation in the world takes place between two or more people who understand what it means to be human. If you are too serious about yourself, you will find that you won't have anybody with whom to be serious.

6

Winning an Argument

Or what king, going to make war against another
king, does not sit down first and consider whether
he is able with ten thousand to meet him who
comes against him with twenty thousand?
Luke 14:31

Have you ever thought about saying something in an
argument—after the argument was already over? Have
you ever expressed an opinion and then been destroyed
by some turkey who felt that her (or his) opinions were the
only correct ones? Have you ever felt the urge to tell someone the truth about his (or her) statements ("That is the
dumbest thing I have ever heard!"), but felt that it just
wouldn't be proper? Have you ever felt embarrassed when
you were in an argument, and got "your lunch eaten"?
Have you ever wished that you could disagree with someone without looking like a fool? If you have ever felt those
frustrations, this is your chapter.

Perhaps you are saying, "This certainly isn't my chapter. I don't argue."

As a matter of fact, if you never argue or debate, you are either a saint, a liar, or you don't have any opinions. The issue of this chapter is not whether or not you argue—we all do, if only in our minds—but whether or not your argumentation is effective. If you only argue in your mind, you will always win, so you don't need any help. But when your argumentation becomes public, this chapter will keep you from making a fool of yourself. As an old hand at making a fool of myself, I've learned some lessons that I've decided to share with you.

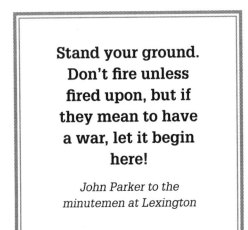

Stand your ground. Don't fire unless fired upon, but if they mean to have a war, let it begin here!

John Parker to the minutemen at Lexington

For the purposes of our discussion, I'm going to divide the chapter into five parts: the warrior mode, choosing the battle, levels of conflict, weapons of war, and cleaning up the battlefield. Let's get to it.

It is important, it seems to me, that before you engage in an argument, whether it is a difference of opinion with a friend or a major conflagration with a "twit," you must first deal with whether or not any argumentation is appropriate—ever.

You will note as you go through this chapter that I use the imagery of warfare. That, I suspect, will be a problem for pacifists and others who feel that "make love, not war" is the only appropriate attitude for a "nice" person. If you are offended by the imagery I use in this chapter, it is a fairly good indication that you probably need what I'm going to teach you here.

In a recent talk show I hosted, I had a verbal debate with one of the callers. The conversation became quite heated. The station lifted that part of the program from the tape and made a promotional spot advertising the program. In the promotional spot, played often during the next week, the announcer said, "Sometimes he laughs and sometimes he gets angry, but he's never dull." Then a few seconds of the taped conversation in which I became angry, followed by, "You don't want to miss Steve on WXYZ."

All that week almost every Christian who loved me enough to tell me what they thought expressed dismay at the spot. As I questioned them about what bothered them, without exception I found that those dear friends felt that there was something wrong with a "religious person" in a heated argument. "Christians," they seemed to be saying, "don't get angry. They don't argue, and they certainly don't do it publicly."

I was astounded at that perception. Nonbelievers who don't like to argue generally say that "It isn't nice," while Christians say "It isn't Christian." Both are wrong. (Christians might want to read my book *No More Mr. Nice Guy*. And you're right, that's a cheap way to sell books.)

John R. W. Stott has written a wonderful book titled *Christ the Controversialist* (InterVarsity Press, 1970). In it he points out that Jesus was constantly engaged in controversy and that many of his discourses were debates with the contemporary Jewish leaders of religion. Jesus was not always "nice" and Christians shouldn't be nice all the time either.

If you aren't a believer, your "niceness" doesn't, of course, have a religious root. However, it does come from the same spurious belief, held by believers and called "Christian," that propriety requires that one never be angry or express strong views. It simply isn't done. In both cases, the idea that controversy is somehow wrong or immoral, is wrong. It is not only wrong, it is also dull—and dullness, for the purposes of this book, is a far greater sin than impropriety.

I got a call recently from a pastor of a rather large church who is one of the finest, most loving, and compassionate pastors I know about anywhere. His problem is that he doesn't have a "mean streak." He told me he was devastated by some very angry and neurotic members of his church who had attacked him and his ministry. "It wouldn't be so bad, Steve," he said, "if it were only me, but they are destroying everything that is worthwhile in the church. Can you help me?"

"No," I said.

"No?"

"No! Because, my friend, you believe that Jesus died to make you nice, and, in this situation, nice simply won't make it. Now, if you are willing to deal with the conflict, face the problem, and straighten out the mess, then I *can* help you. But as long as you insist on being a pussycat, instead of the lion that God called you to be, I can't help. I'm not into training kittens."

This man knew that I loved him, and he accepted what I said with the grace with which he also accepted (but should not have) the attacks of people who were trying to destroy the wonderful ministry he had in that church. He didn't like anything I told him to do, but he did it because he was in trouble and knew it. Today he has a strong, viable, and exciting ministry that is touching a whole lot of people.

The point is this: More than half of his battle was in deciding that it was appropriate to have a battle. After that was settled in his mind, he was able to do what needed to be done.

If you truly believe that one should never argue or disagree with others, nothing I say beyond this point is going to help you. You can save yourself a lot of time by going to the next chapter—assuming, of course, that you don't have a moral problem with giving a speech. You see, the first step in winning an argument is beginning to see yourself in the warrior mode.

You are a valuable person with views that are sound and good. You will be right (assuming the law of averages) at least 50 percent of the time. Neither the Bible nor common sense suggests that you should fade into the background and become a doormat. Get that straight in your mind, and you are closer to the goal than you think.

With all of the above being said, I am not for a moment suggesting that you become a critical, argumentative, and angry person. Jesus got angry—but he was not angry most of the time. While it is important that you be willing to assume a warrior mode, you must choose your battles very carefully.

You have not been called to straighten out the world, to correct every stupid comment made in your presence, to remedy every spurious theological, philosophical, or political view, or to be everyone's mother. There are some arguments you can win and some in which you should never participate. Before you argue, disagree with, or challenge anyone about anything, ask yourself, "Is it worth it?"

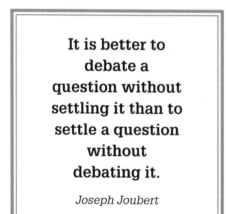

> **It is better to debate a question without settling it than to settle a question without debating it.**
>
> *Joseph Joubert*

For instance, if you don't feel strongly about an issue, just let it go. If the person with whom you are planning an argu-

> ## There is nothing so annoying as arguing with a person who knows what he's talking about.
>
> *Anonymous*

ment is so convinced that he or she is right that no mind change is possible, then you are foolish to try. It is stupid to engage in an argument on economics, for instance, if you can't balance your checkbook. There are times when engaging in an argument is not brave—it is idiotic (arguing with your boss, wife, or husband).

So, in argumentation, always choose your battle carefully. Ask yourself, "What is this battle going to cost me [and others] if I win the argument?" "What is it going to cost me (and others) if I lose it?" There are times when the cost of the argument can be too high to pay. Counting the cost before you buy the product is a good practice in a department store, before going into a marriage, and before engaging in an argument.

Thirdly, it is terribly important that you recognize the different levels of conflict in an argument. Each level of conflict requires a different mode of battle. Don't go after a flea with a howitzer. Just so, an argument with a spouse or a friend is quite different from an argument with someone who is trying to destroy you.

There are four levels of conflict—and one exception. Let me give them to you.

Level One: Argument Without an Enemy

Remember this principle: A relationship does not move from an acquaintance to a friendship without sparks. The deeper the relationship, the more possibility for argument. In everyday relationships there is always disagreement and, thus, argument. The difference between an argument within a relationship of marriage, friendship, or with co-workers is that the object is not to win the argument, to prove a point, and certainly not to get your way. The goal in this kind of setting is to strengthen and deepen the relationship.

Ruth Graham was once asked if she and Dr. Graham ever disagreed. Her reply was classic: "Of course. If we didn't, there would be no need for one of us." That is true in every family, every workplace, and every friendship. The question is what to do when the argument is with someone you care about. Let me give you eight rules that can make a difference:

Rule 1. *Never characterize the argument made by someone you love.* Repeat what he or she said and try to be as accurate as you can possibly be.

Rule 2. *Keep short accounts. Always clean up the mess promptly lest one argument lead to another.* The Bible says, "Don't let the sun go down on your anger." That is an important admonition when feeling anger toward someone with whom you are close.

Rule 3. *Keep "weapons of destruction" in the closet.* A "weapon of destruction" is when you bring to the battle weapons that have nothing to do with the battle at hand. A husband will say to his wife, "I think you are wrong about this car you think we should buy [clearly stated opinion], and you are also a horrible cook (weapon of destruction)." Or she says to him, "I know you don't agree, but I think it is important that we invite the Smiths to dinner [clearly stated terms of argument]. Do you know something else?

You were lousy in bed last night" (weapon of destruction).

A sound relationship can stand any argument, but using weapons of destruction will always weaken and destroy relationships.

Rule 4. *Apologize quickly.*

Rule 5. *Affirm easily.*

Rule 6. *Compromise often.*

Rule 7. *Stick to issues.* As long as the discussion/argument is objective, the issues can be settled. Once the argument degenerates into characterizing your spouse, friend, or co-worker as "stupid" for his or her views on the issues, you have made a mess that is hard to clean up.

Rule 8. *Look for points of agreement and concentrate on them as you branch out to settle the issue.*

In an argument or a disagreement with someone with whom you have an important relationship, the only reason for the argument or the disagreement is to reach some kind of accord so that you can walk hand in hand with that accord to a particular goal. Winning arguments with people who are important to you is always a losing strategy. Remember, the relationship is always more important than any argument.

Level Two: Argument When You Don't Want an Enemy

I was a pastor for a long time. One of the reasons I'm glad I am no longer a pastor is that I am no longer everybody's mother. I learned some good lessons, however, while a pastor, and one of the best ones is this: Mothers have the power to destroy their children—but good mothers don't do that. You can win an argument and lose a person. The church, like any institution, has a certain number of neurotics in its midst. There are people who are narrow, critical, and destructive. I am good at polemics and can usually win an argument. Sometimes, however, by winning an argument, I can hurt the church, destroy the ministry, and give great pain to someone to whom God has sent me as a pastor.

I once locked an elder in my study and yelled at him until he agreed with me. Do you know what happened? He left the church. I worked hard on restoring our relationship and was reasonably successful. I asked forgiveness and I went out of my way to let him know about my shame over what I had done. He forgave me and we became friends—but he never came back to the church.

Let me tell you a story. A number of years ago there was an Episcopal bishop by the name of James Pike who began to go through a crisis of faith. He eventually resigned from the Episcopate and began a search for some answers in spiritualism and the occult. Bishop Pike's son's death was the great tragedy of his life and, through a spiritualist medium, he felt that he had contacted his son.

On one occasion Bishop Pike engaged in a major public forum with a prominent theologian who was an excellent polemicist. I am told that it wasn't much of a debate. The theologian literally decimated every argument of Bishop Pike until even those who were not sympathetic to Pike's arguments felt sorry for him.

Toward the end of his life, Pike engaged in another public debate, this time with the late theologian and writer Francis Schaeffer, who was then the head of L'Abri, a Christian fellowship in Switzerland. L'Abri was and is a place where people with honest questions could get honest answers.

During the debate Schaeffer was clearly the better of the two in terms of argument. He was plainly more knowledgeable and articulate than Pike. But Dr. Schaeffer refused to "go for the jugular." Schaeffer would make his points with clarity, show what he saw as some of the inconsistencies of Pike's arguments, and then would affirm Pike and agree with him in those few places where agreement could be found.

Now let me tell you the rest of the story. After the first debate, Pike was driven further and further from his Christian roots. But on the day when James Pike died, he had been making plans to go to Switzerland where he planned to learn under the teaching of Francis Schaeffer.

Schaeffer, you see, had an enemy but made him a friend.

That is true with a lot of argumentation. Of course, there are some people you would rather have as an enemy than a friend. A man was dying and knew it. He called his wife to his bedside and said, "Call your brother and tell him that I forgive him. But wait until after I'm dead—and you're sure I'm dead." Sometimes you want an enemy to stay that way, but when you are not only trying to win an argument but also trying to make a friend, you must be very careful.

Utilize, with a bit more harshness, the rules I gave you above when you are arguing at Level One.

Level Three: Argument with an Enemy

There are always arguments in which there is a definable adversary, someone who has clearly drawn the battle lines, refuses to compromise, and is determined to destroy you and your argument. These kinds of disagreements almost always revolve around issues—political, theological, philosophical—and must be handled carefully and deftly.

Nick Thornely and Dan Lees's book, *Winning with Words*, has a very good warning: "Winners with words almost never use their full powers, but there are some verbal battles which are like street fights in which even a mas-

ter may be compelled to employ a few crippling blows."
(Mercury Books, London, 1991, p. 145)

This level of argument is a "street fight" where one gives
no quarter and takes no prisoners. There will always be,
especially if one is a Christian, the necessity of cleaning up
after the battle. We will deal with that later. But, for now,
know that there are some people who are out to "eat your
lunch." Only the very naive and superficial miss the signals.

Level Four: Argument with an Angry/Vindictive Enemy

This is an argument with the kind of person who would
just as soon come after you with a knife or a gun as with
words. When the attack comes, it is apparent that it goes
far beyond a mere argument or debate. This is the kind of
person who, for whatever reason, "hates your guts" and
is bent on destroying you. Mercifully, this kind of
encounter doesn't happen often, but it does happen, and
it is important to recognize it when it happens.

I was once speaking at a conference where a man I had
never met before approached me with fire in his eyes. He
immediately started yelling at me about something I had
said. Sometimes if you are quiet, this kind of person will blow
off steam and when it is finally out, calm down. But, in this
case, the more the man shouted at me, the louder he became.
The whole thing was fast developing into what might be a
physical attack. It ended when a friend of mine (a very *big*
friend) intervened and gently escorted the man off.

Those kinds of things happen. When they do, there are
three very important rules:

1. Don't argue.
2. Don't argue.
3. Don't argue.

Arguing with someone like that is like trying to teach a lion to eat watermelon. The lion's nature is to dislike melon, and the more you force it on the lion, the more angry the lion will get. Best just to walk away. (If your angry adversary is big, you might want to run.)

My friend Ed Pope is the sports editor of *The Miami Herald*. When Ed gets critical letters, he has a standard response: "Dear so and so. You may be right. Sincerely, Ed Pope." I have learned to answer most critical letters the same way but with a twist. "Dear so and so, You may be right . . . *but you are probably wrong*. Sincerely, Steve Brown." The point is to get away from the person quickly, and with as much grace as possible.

Of course, there are some occasions when you simply can't walk away. When that happens, stand your ground and use what I'm going to teach you about the weapons of war. Sometimes bullies wilt when confronted. Sometimes they don't. Either way, you will do well to "watch your backside."

Addendum: Argument Before an Audience

Sometimes those listening to an argument are more important to you than the person with whom you are arguing. A number of years ago I was invited to debate the atheist, Madalyn Murray O'Hair, on a television show. I refused, not because I would lose the debate (I would have at least come out even), but because I was aware of the audience we would have. I had watched O'Hair's debating technique. She is angry, caustic, bitter, and scathing. To win a debate with O'Hair, one must become what she is and match her invective with invective.

At the time of the invitation, I was a pastor and realized that many Christians would be watching. There was no way I could win the debate without engaging in the kind of polemics for which Mrs. O'Hair was famous. If I had done that, I would have betrayed the essence of my position. In other words, I would have had to become something that violated the loving and irenic demeanor required of a pastor. I was more concerned about the audience than I was about Mrs. O'Hair and winning the debate with her.

Whenever there is an audience to an argument or debate, whether the audience is one or a thousand, that adds another factor to the debate. There are occasions when I am challenged on a college campus or when speaking at a conference. If the challenge is made one on one, I can afford to be kind, back off, and deal with it as a friendly joust. However, the challenge is usually made when an audience is present. Because of that audience and the importance of maintaining the credibility of my message, it is important that I win the argument and that I do it quickly, even if the challenger is hurt.

Be aware of your audience. If you are arguing with a drug pusher about drugs and there are any kids watching, or if you are arguing about ethics and there are business people listening, or if you are arguing about the value of persons and there are people with poor self-images listening—go to Level Three very quickly and act according to those rules.

Planning to Win

Now, having set the parameters, I move to the next question: How do you *win* an argument?

Weapons

I want to tell you about the ten weapons that winners of arguments always utilize. I suggest that you

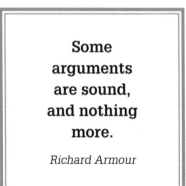

Some arguments are sound, and nothing more.

Richard Armour

work in these areas if you want to become an effective polemicist. Anybody who engages in an argument without using the right weapons is going to end up on the short end of the confabulational stick.

Because this, of course, is not a book devoted entirely to logic and argumentation, by necessity I must limit the ways to argue to some very basic and simple methodologies. If you are interested in going into this further, there are a number of books in your local library which will pursue the subject in far more detail.

The first weapon is *knowledge*. The rule is this: Never get in an argument on a subject about which you know nothing. The corollary of that rule is this: When you find yourself in an argument and realize that you don't know what you are talking about, the best policy is to admit your lack of knowledge and retreat from the argument.

I know a lot about theology. I am familiar with the arguments for the existence of God, the reality of the supernatural, and the absolute nature of morals. I can win almost all of those arguments. I am reasonably informed in politics, philosophy and social ethics, so I can hold my own in those kinds of arguments. But if I should argue about science, economics, or the arts, my best defense is humility and silence.

The second weapon is *clarity*. It does you no good to know a lot if you can't say it in a way that your adversary and your audience can understand. There is one very important technique that can help you clarify your knowledge for the purposes of debate. Always practice expressing your thoughts before friends—under the rubric that it is important to run the flag up a friendly flagpole to see if anyone salutes before you run the flag up a hostile flagpole. For instance, I usually invite criticism of what I say and the views I express from those with whom I am close. My wife, daughters, and staff will often tell me a better way to say something. And my editor, Steve Griffith, is always helping me to say something better and with more clarity.

The third weapon is **practice**. Someone once asked his mentor in business to what he attributed his phenomenal success. He replied, "Making good decisions."

"Well," the young man said, "how did you learn to make good decisions?"

"Bad decisions."

It's the same way with argumentation. If you never express opposing views and never have your views knocked down, you will never learn to express views that will stand the test of argumentation.

My brother was a lawyer and a very good one. Early in his practice, he went for a number of months without losing a case in court. But finally the inevitable came, and he lost his first case.

Later, he was having lunch with some friends who were kidding him about losing his first court battle. My brother's comment was wise and funny. He said, "Gentlemen, yesterday I lost my virginity, but I have no intentions of becoming a prostitute." He was saying, "I have learned from my failure—and there will be another day and another time when I will put what I have learned into practice."

I think I am a reasonably good polemicist. I win most arguments in which I find myself. But I can't tell you the number of times that I have been bloodied in the heat of argumentation. Every time I made a fool of myself, every time I lost an argument, every time I said something stupid and banal, I learned something about the art of argument.

So, take risks. Express your views, accept challenges, and lose graciously. Before long you will improve. The problem is that you can't get from where you are to where you want to go without some significant failures along the way. Someone has said that the difference between a successful person and a failure is that the successful person got up the last time he or she was knocked down. That is true in learning to win arguments too.

The fourth weapon is *control*. More arguments have been lost by uncontrolled emotions, especially anger, than for any other reason. William Buckley is one of my heroes. I love to watch him engage in debate. He almost always wins. A number of years ago, Buckley was on a television program with Gore Vidal, and Vidal (a rather irritating person anyway) called Buckley a "crypto-Nazi." Buckley became quite angry and called Vidal a "queer." It was one of the few times that Buckley lost an argument.

The English say, "Don't get mad—get even." That may not be very "nice," but it *is* effective. Controlled anger will sharpen your focus, hone your argument, and provide great power for your words—as long as it is controlled.

Learn to count to ten. Learn to ask questions when you feel like attacking. Learn to challenge quietly and authoritatively. Learn to pour water, not gasoline, on the fire. You can always tell who is losing an argument by checking out who is yelling the loudest.

The fifth weapon is *challenge*. Always be quick to ask a person with whom you are arguing to cite his or her sources of authority. This practice keeps your opponent honest. (While you are doing this, make sure that you can authenticate your own sources.) People who don't know what they are talking about are often given to pontificating with statistics, quotes, and esoteric bits of information. It is always a good practice to say, "Madam [Sir], that is the silliest thing I have ever heard. Cite your sources!"

A word of caution here: If you are sure that what the other person is saying is spurious, you can challenge with great authority, in the full knowledge that there are *no* credible sources. However, if you aren't sure, a little humility will be helpful. In the latter case one could say, "You may be right, but I have a hard time believing it. Do you have any authority for saying that? If you do, I would be interested in hearing where you got the information."

The sixth weapon is **universalizing.** Kant, on the subject of ethics, suggested that one of the best ways to determine that an action was ethical was to think about what would happen if the contemplated action became universal. In other words, if what I am thinking about doing were to be done by everyone, what would be the result? In argumentation (as well as ethics), universalizing is an important weapon.

For instance, if someone is advocating what you believe are extravagant sums for entitlement programs, go to the wall with your argument by saying, "What happens if more people are receiving money from entitlement programs than there are people putting money into the programs?" Or, if you are a capitalist and are debating a socialist, you can make a telling point by mentioning what happens when a vampire starts living off his own blood. Or, if you are a Christian and are debating the absolute nature of ethical standards, describe what would happen if *nobody* observed absolute standards.

A variation of this theme is the use of exaggeration. Almost every spurious argument clearly will be shown to be spurious when the argument is taken to the extreme, and a question is asked as to what would happen if we *all* accepted it as truth.

One time Walter Martin was in a debate on a New York radio program with an atheist who had a Jewish background. The man had said that all values of any society were, and should be, relative to the society in which they are found. In other words, values are determined by vote. Martin said that if he had had the time, he could have dealt with the argument in a detailed and sophisticated way. But there were time constraints and it was important that he make his point effectively and quickly.

"Let's play pretend," Martin said to his adversary when they had returned to the air from a commercial break. "Let's pretend that we are living in Germany under the Third Reich and I am in the SS. Let's further pretend that my colleagues have just rousted you, a Jew, out of your bed at night and taken you down to headquarters, and that I now have a German Luger pointed at your head. Now, you tell me why I shouldn't pull the trigger."

All of a sudden, what had been a discussion became a reality, and a frightening one at that. The atheist said, "You can't do that."

"Why?" asked Martin.

"Because it's wrong."

"It's not wrong. You yourself said that values are determined by the society in which they are found. We as a society have determined that you are part of an inferior race and should be destroyed. Why shouldn't I pull the trigger?"

By the time the atheist had gotten his act together, Martin had won the argument. If there are no absolute values, then love is as good as hate, destroying life as good as preserving it, and stealing as good as earning. If there were no absolute values, then Hitler and a thousand other major and minor tyrants could have a field day as long as they could convince their constituency that what they are saying is right.

If you are a believer engaged in a religious argument, very few of your adversaries can live with the skewed logic of their arguments. For instance, in debating the subject of the ultimate end of those who are evil, make the point that retribution is God's testament to man's responsibility. If Albert Schweitzer and Adolf Hitler get the same reward, something is skewed in the universe, and we can ascertain that the universe is meaningless. Meaninglessness is a nice topic for debate, but very few people can live with its stark reality. If the universe is meaningless, then the person with whom you are debating isn't important and what he or she does to define himself or herself has no ultimate meaning. Suicide becomes the only option.

This is not a course in Logic 101, but you do need to remember that most sophistry will be revealed as sophistry when one analyzes the argument and applies it to real life situations.

The seventh weapon is *humility*. Pool hustlers win at pool, not necessarily because they are so good, but because they have convinced their opponents that they are not so good. That is true in good argument too. Not only that, it is sometimes honest humility. There is always the possibility, no matter how articulate and knowledgeable you are about any subject, that there is someone who knows more than you know about it, can talk better than you, and can bloody you in battle. Don't go into an argument with the attitude of a braggart. If you lose, you will feel even more the fool.

It is always wise to exercise a little humility. It provides a good way of escape if you get into trouble, and it also throws your opponent off. If you know your material and can articulate it well, don't brag about it—just do it. When you don't know something, be quick to laugh and say, "I don't know." If you are wrong, admit it quickly. If you have made a mistake, don't ever try to cover it. Pascal said, "Do you wish men to speak well of you? Then never speak well of yourself."

The eighth weapon is *humor*. Not everyone is capable of utilizing this weapon well, but, if you have the gift, use it effectively. A well-timed humorous story or line can win an audience, defuse an opponent's good point and, in the meantime, give you a chance to collect your thoughts.

Casey Stengel was once being heckled by a woman in the stands. She shouted out, "Stengel, if I were married to you, I would feed you poison."

Stengel yelled back, "And if I were married to you, I would take it."

Along the same line, Churchill was once admonished by a woman because he was drunk. "Mr. Prime Minister," she said in a dignified but angry way, "you are drunk."

"You are right," replied Churchill, "but, madam, *you* are ugly. Tomorrow morning, *I* will be sober."

The ninth weapon is *recapitulation*. It is always wise to repeat an opponent's argument, and in the repetition, eliminate pejorative words and add your own. If, for instance, someone has said, "Charity always begins at home, and we have no business taking our hard-earned dollars and feeding the shiftless bums who refuse to work or be productive members of society," you would repeat the argument being made like this: "Let me make sure that I understand what you are saying. Am I right in hearing you say that poor people must be kept poor?"

The tenth weapon should be used only sparingly—never if it can be avoided. The weapon is *dismissal*. This occurs when one dismisses an opponent's argument as if it were ridiculous and totally without merit. The danger of using dismissal is that it has a tendency to dismiss the person as well as the argument and no ethical polemicist will devalue a person to win an argument.

Recapitulation consists of saying something like, "I won't dignify such drivel by replying to it!" or, "What you have just said is so silly and superficial that it deserves no reply." One of the best ways to use this weapon is to simply ignore your opponent's argument.

Battlefield Cleanup

Before we move to the next chapter, it is important to say a word about cleaning up the battlefield. In any battle there are bodies to be removed, wounds to be bandaged, and the psychologically traumatized to be treated. In all

> **Nothing except a battle lost can be half as melancholy as a battle won.**
>
> *Duke of Wellington*

arguments, with the exception of Level One (and sometimes even then), there is always a lot of damage to repair. What can you do about that? There are three rules to remember.

The first rule is to never gloat over a victory. There is nothing worse for relationships than to win an argument and then celebrate your victory under the nose of your opponent. More often than not, arguments are much ado about nothing. In the give-and-take of ideas, sometimes you win and sometimes you lose. It is harder to be humble and gracious when you win than when you lose—but it is far more important.

The second rule is to always praise your opponent. The debating style of Cal Thomas, the conservative columnist, is one of the finest examples of effective argumentation I know. He made an appearance once on a talk show in Miami and, for almost two hours, absolutely decimated the liberal-minded host. At the end of the program, Cal said, "I want to thank you for having me on your program. As you know, I am a guest on hundreds of talk shows, and I must say that you are one of the best prepared and most articulate hosts I have yet encountered. I appreciate your allowing me to be a part of your show." Cal will be invited back. But, more important than that, he "valued" and respected his opponent.

There is no one living who hasn't felt like a fool on occasion, who has not been embarrassed by his or her own words, or who has not lost a number of arguments. Remember how you felt when that happened, and make sure that you bind up the wounds that you would want to be bound up had you been in the place of your opponent. I am not suggesting that you be dishonest in your praise. However, I am suggesting that you look carefully for something to praise and that you give it.

The third and final rule is to sometimes lose. You don't have to win every argument. Only secure people can lose an argument on purpose. But there are lots of things in this world that are far more important than winning an argument. People are more important; love and relationships are more important; certainly, the affirmation of another person's worth is more important.

On the other hand, I don't really have to give you that rule. You *will* sometimes lose an argument—although you will probably lose fewer arguments now that you have read this chapter.

7

A Flower for Your Consideration

The preparations of the heart belong to man, but
the answer of the tongue is from the Lord.
Prov. 16:1

If you want to give a speech, this is the most important chapter in the book. That doesn't mean you don't have to read beyond this chapter (there is some good stuff ahead), but if you want the essence of what it takes to speak well publicly, you will find it here.

If you are familiar with theology, you have probably heard of John Calvin. If you are familiar with Calvin, you are aware that Calvin's theology is often distilled into what has been called, "The Five Points of Calvinism." If you are familiar with the Five Points of Calvinism, you are probably aware that the modern form in which those points are presented is the form of an acrostic. If you know that, you know the acrostic is TULIP.

I have five points to make about speechmaking. Not only that, these five points of communication can be remembered with the help of an acrostic, and the acrostic is also TULIP.

One of the difficulties with most books on public speaking is that they are so detailed and complicated that, by the time you become proficient in doing all that is suggested, you are too old to give a speech. In teaching "communication" to theological students, I have found that it is very important to focus on a few essential principles.

For a number of years I taught swimming and diving. I remember one young man who wanted to learn to dive. I told him, "Billy, if your head is right, everything else will be fine."

Billy did his first dive and when he came out of the water, he asked, "Mr. Brown, did I keep my legs together?"

"Billy," I said, "don't worry about your legs. Remember what I said about your head."

Then he tried again, and his dive still looked something like a dying chicken. "Mr. Brown," he asked, his stomach red from the belly flop, "was my approach right?"

"Billy, forget about your approach. Worry about your head. Forget the rest. If your head is right, the rest will be okay."

In the TULIP of communication, I want to teach you the five most important elements in making a speech or any kind of public presentation. If you get this right, even though everything else is wrong, you will be reasonably successful. If you get this wrong, and everything else in this book or any other book on speech right, you will never give a speech that will cause people to listen.

Let's get to it.

Therapeutic

The first element of any good presentation is that it must be "Therapeutic" (from a Greek word meaning "servant" or "attendant"). In other words, a speech must have a purpose in mind that will prove helpful to the people to whom you are making a presentation.

If you are a pastor, you must remember that no one cares about the Graf-Wellhausen documentary hypothesis, whether or not your Lapsarian view is proper, or how Augustine differs from Aquinas. The people in the pews are dying. They are worried about their families, their jobs, and their futures. They feel guilty and afraid. They aren't even sure that God exists, and if he does, what difference it makes.

> **Eloquence is the language of nature, and cannot be learned in the schools; but rhetoric is the creature of art, which he who feels least will most excel in.**
>
> *Charles Caleb Colton*

Frederick Buechner, in the second volume of his autobiography, *Now and Then*, tells about the time he had just been called to be the minister at Exeter Boys' School. He writes about his preaching experience, quoting from Karl Barth and including Barth's assertion that people come to church because they want to believe that what is said is true:

> I have never assumed that the people I talk to are so certain
> . . . that the question is not still very much alive for them. Is
> anyone ever that certain? I assume always that they want to
> know if it is true as much as I do myself. I assume that even
> the most religiously disillusioned and negative among them
> want it to be true as much as the relatively devout do—want
> to be shown it, want it to be made somehow flesh before
> their eyes, want to be able to rejoice in it for themselves. And

it is because, at some level of their being, their wanting is so great that you must be so careful what you give them, and because your wanting to give is so great, too. (*Now and Then*, San Francisco: Harper & Row, 1983, p. 70)

In other words, the focus of any public presentation is the audience. If you forget them, no matter how impressive you are, your message won't make it to the first row. Always ask, "What difference will this make?" If you can't find an answer, don't give the speech.

I don't know about you, but I grow tired of people giving a speech when a written report would have done just as well. Much time is wasted on verbal presentations that just don't have any relevance for listeners. The most important gift an audience will give you is their time. Once they give it, make sure that you don't waste it by telling them something they don't need.

Always, before preparing a presentation, ask what purpose you are trying to achieve. That purpose must serve the audience or your presentation is wasted.

Unconventional

The second of the five points is "Unconventional." We live in an age that bombards us with words. Everywhere we turn there are people vying for our attention. To be an effective communicator, you must do something or say something that will make others want to listen to what you have to say.

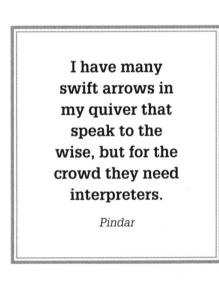

I have many swift arrows in my quiver that speak to the wise, but for the crowd they need interpreters.

Pindar

I often tell my students that if they think they shouldn't say something, they probably should. Whenever you think, "This is a little too strong," it probably isn't. Even if you feel that what you are going to say might offend your audience, you probably ought to say it anyway. It is better to offend people than to put them to sleep.

I have a preacher friend who brought his dog into the pulpit to demonstrate discipleship. That was a major risk, but nobody slept, and he made his point. Think in terms of graphics—the use of an overhead, posters, or other visual representations of your words. For instance, one motivational speaker makes a point on perspective by pouring water into a glass while he is talking. When the glass is about half full, he asks, "Do you think this glass is half empty or half full?"

For a number of years I have struggled with ways to get people to listen to what I was saying in my sermons. During a very difficult year of my life, I developed a hip problem which required me to sit down when I preached. I generally had a stool in place of the pulpit.

During those months when the pain required me to use the stool, I noticed that people were listening more intently than they had before. Then it began to dawn on me that, by sitting, my sermons seemed less "preachy" and threatening. I noticed that people relaxed a bit more than before. By the time the pain had subsided, I had developed a new way of preaching: sitting on a stool. The church I was serving at that time had theater seats and was in the round. One of the elders of the church responding to a friend's comment that so many people were coming to church said, "No wonder. Our pastor sits on a bar stool and the people sit in theater seats."

Humor, when used appropriately, can make a difference by breaking out of the conventional mold. I was once speaking at Ben Haden's church in Chattanooga. If you are famil-

iar with Ben and his preaching style on television, you know
that he, being a former lawyer paces as he preaches, almost
as if he were making a presentation to a jury. A lady was
quite incensed at my style. She walked out muttering, "We
have a preacher who walks and talks and he invites one
who sits and laughs. I'm tired of it." Well, she may have
been tired of it, but she didn't go to sleep either.

I have a friend who kept turning the lectern light off and
on during his presentation. Toward the end of his speech,
he said, "You have probably wondered why I have been
turning this light on and off while I was talking to you. I
have done it to cause you to ask that question and also to
keep you from drifting."

How you use words can be unconventional too. Once you
have decided on the key sentences that communicate the
message, try to rewrite the sentence in a way that will amuse,
shock, astound, or colorfully picture what you are saying.
For instance, when making a report about some statistics
that point to a significant trend in your company, if you say,
"I have noticed that there is an interesting trend here,"
people will continue to sleep. Instead, say, "Now, I have
something exciting to show you. If you've been drifting, it's
time you listen up! These statistics will astound you."

Using words like "Listen up!" or "Some of you have
been sleeping, and I know your names," can cause people
to stay with you. I have often used an existential question
to keep people listening for an answer, such as, "Have you
ever wondered if God was a monster?" Sometimes a whisper or a shout will do it.

I am fond of using words that are unconventional like
"balderdash," or "twit," or "turkey" or "horse feathers!"
On one occasion I was approached by an elder of a church
where I was the pastor. He said, "Pastor, I really do like
your sermons, but I wish you would quit using 'horse
feathers!' One of these days you are going to slip."

I don't know which agency thought up the name "Fudd-ruckers" for the hamburger and hot dog chain, but who-ever did (along with "Granny Feel Good's" and "T.G.I.F.") is a genius. He or she understood the necessity of being unconventional.

If you are "different," people will listen. If you talk like everyone else, you'll get lost in the crowd.

Lucidity

The third point of communication is "Lucidity." Let me give you another principle: If people can't take notes on what you say, you should not have said it. Now I don't mean that everyone should take notes on what you said, but if people wanted to, and couldn't, it is a good indication that your thoughts were not organized clearly and your message fell on deaf ears.

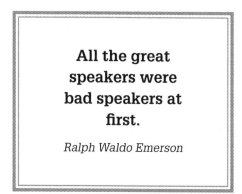

All the great speakers were bad speakers at first.

Ralph Waldo Emerson

I'll have more to say about this in the next chapter, but, for now, let me say that organization is des-perately important in any presentation. The points should be numbered, and the number should be mentioned, often with a reference to what has gone on before. For instance, *"First,* I talked about the power of motivation, and *second,* I want to talk about personifying the motivation. . . ."

When you are making a transition, don't assume that people will follow you. They won't unless you make clear reference to your transition. Most good presentations have one main thrust and a number of subheadings under that idea. Make sure that the main theme is clear in your own mind before you try to make it clear in the minds of others. Ask yourself what you are trying to accomplish in your presentation. If you can't say in one sentence what you are trying to accomplish, then you won't achieve it.

Illustrate

The fourth point of communication is "Illustrate." It is said that Sydney Smith, the British clergyman and author who helped found the *Edinburgh Review*, was once praying out loud. A friend overheard him say, "Now, Lord, I'll tell you an anecdote."

It is possible, I suppose, that the Lord didn't want to hear the anecdote or that He was even offended—but I doubt it. You see, when He gave us His book, He didn't give us a list of doctrines, a confessional statement, a systematic theology, and an index. That's what we gave Him, and getting to the truth isn't a half bad gift to give to God. When He gave us His book, He gave us a book with many illustrations because He created people who like and respond to stories.

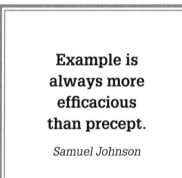

Example is always more efficacious than precept.

Samuel Johnson

An effective communicator is a clever illustrator. A good principle is this: If you can't illustrate it, it isn't true or it doesn't matter. Now this doesn't mean that every point you make must be accompanied by an illustration. There is a danger (into which I often fall) of having too many illustrations. However, you should be able (even if you don't) to give an illustration for every point you make.

My mentor John Stanton used to tell me that the problem with my early sermons was that they had no "windows." He explained that illustrations were the windows by which people could see the application or the truth of what one was teaching. I will be eternally grateful for his advice in this area. He taught me to tell a story that would apply truth and make everything I said practical.

Where does one get illustrations? Dr. Donald Grey Barnhouse said, "All of life illustrates Bible doctrine." He was right, but the principle is even broader than that. One could say that "all of life illustrates truth" because it does, and a good public speaker will be attuned to life in terms of illustrations of truth. If you are making a motivational presentation to employees about the importance of focusing on the customer and meeting the customer's needs, you must illustrate that principle with actual accounts of how success has been achieved by that practice. If you simply state the truth, it will soon be forgotten.

Most illustrations come from life and by being sensitive to it. Bishop William Quayle once gave a sermon for preachers in which he named observation as one of the major tasks of a preacher. He said:

When this preacher comes to a Sunday in his journey through the week, people ask him, "Preacherman, where were you and what saw you while the workmen were sweating at their toil?" And then of this preacher we may say reverently, "He opened his mouth and taught them saying": and there will be another, though lesser, Sermon on the Mount. And the auditors sit and sob and shout under their breast, and say with their helped hearts, "Preacher, saw you and heard you that? You were well employed. Go

out and listen and look another week; but be very sure to
come back and tell us what you heard and saw."

Every encounter with real people—every hurt expressed, every occupation observed, every life lived—provides illustrative material for speechmakers. Someone has
said that the art of writing is the art of observation. That's
as true for a speaker as it is for a writer. Anyone can write
a sentence, punctuate correctly, and use a dictionary to
spell properly, but only those who observe life have anything meaningful to say.

While you are observing others, don't forget to observe
yourself. If you are a preacher, remember that you cannot
comment on the human race as an outsider. Airports don't
have separate bathrooms for men, women, and clergymen.
After some twenty-eight years as a pastor, I have discovered that the things that frighten, tempt, and inspire me,
also frighten, tempt, and inspire everyone else. As a result,
I have found that one of the greatest sources of illustrations is myself and what is going on in my own life.

Another way to find illustrations is, of course, by reading. The communicator who doesn't read is going to be in
some serious trouble. You ask, "What should I read?"
Everything. Read the advertising on cereal boxes, read bill-
boards, read magazines, and read every book you can get
your hands on.

And don't forget television and radio. I am weary of
speakers who are constantly on the warpath with the electronic media. Let me tell you a secret: No industry is more
sensitive to what people want than commercial broadcasting. It exists solely by finding out what people want
and then giving it to them. I don't like that any more than
you do, but it is a fact. So the speaker who is not aware of
what the electronic media are doing is going to miss the
real "place" where people live. One of the best sources of
illustrative material is television and radio.

Another source of illustrative material is books of illustrations. I know. I know. It sounds like cheating, but it really isn't as long as you give credit to the person who first told the story or used the illustration. Most "illustration books" are not very good, but if you get three or four good examples from a book, it is worth the price of the book.

Now let me give you the best resource I know for illustrations: the people to whom you speak. When you make it clear to your audiences that you would "sell your soul" for a good illustration, those dear folks will become your research assistants. Not only that, they will enjoy hearing a story or quote they have given you, which will increase their desire to give you more. Speaking is never a private affair. It should involve the audience, and one of the best ways to do that is to ask them to help you with finding illustrations.

> **The union of the mathematician with the poet, fervor with measure, passion with correctness, this surely is the ideal.**
>
> *William James*

Passion

The fifth and final point of communication is "Passion." If it doesn't matter to you, it won't matter to anyone else!

I hate dull, lifeless, and passionless presentations. In fact, I have decided that I will never listen to one again. When I am forced to sit through a colorless presentation, I play a game. I try to see if the speaker used all the letters of the alphabet, and then count how many times I can go through the alphabet before he finishes by using only the first letters of words used in the presentation. I was able once to get through the alphabet four times. That, I know, was not very respectful, but it was a whole lot more courteous than falling asleep.

If you are a preacher, it is difficult to take something as exciting as the Gospel and make it dull. Yet, you and I know that it happens in thousands of churches every Sunday morning. If you are a salesman with a product that doesn't engender a contagious excitement in your heart and mind, you ought to get another product. And if your presentation to a board or a committee doesn't "turn you on" it's a sure bet that it won't move anyone else either.

My friend John Haggai, the founder and director of the Haggai Institute for Advanced Leadership Training, is one of the most effective communicators I know. He is also one of the most effective fund-raisers I have ever known. Once, when I was trying to raise money for a building program, I called John up and asked him how he did it.

He said, "Steve, I tell my secretary to hold all my calls and that—short of the second coming of Christ—I don't want to be interrupted. Then I sit behind my desk and think about the project on which I am working and the difference it is going to make in people's lives. When I am so excited that I can't sit there anymore, I go out and ask for money."

That can work with your speech too. As you are working on it, get excited about it. If you can't get excited about it, ask someone else to take your place.

8

Preparing a Speech

Preach the word! Be ready in season and out of season. Convince, rebuke, exhort, with all
longsuffering and teaching.
2 Tim. 4:2

I had a professor in seminary who told his students that
for every minute preachers spend in the pulpit, they ought
to spend an hour in preparation.

He was a fruitcake. Not only that, he had not served a
church in twenty years and had no idea of the time
demands on a busy pastor today. Many pastors give three
thirty-minute sermons a week and, following my professor's admonishment, he or she would have to spend ninety
hours in preparation. That's fine if you're a monk, don't
have a family, and don't want to eat and sleep.

While that professor was wrong about the amount of time
one needs to spend in sermon preparation, he was not wrong
about the importance of preparation. As Louis Pasteur once
said, "Chance favors only the mind that is prepared."

President Nixon once told me that while talking to Winston Churchill's son, he told him how much he admired the prime minister's great ability at giving "extemporaneous" speeches. Churchill's son replied, "Oh, yes, I've watched my father work for hours preparing those extemporaneous speeches."

One mark of a good speech is the effortlessness with which it is delivered. There is a direct correlation between the effortlessness with which one delivers a speech and the preparation that went into putting the speech together. I have a friend who loves to give speeches, but he's not very good at it. I overheard him say to a mutual friend, "I don't prepare. I guess I just have the gift."

I wanted to say (but didn't) that he did have a gift, but it wasn't for making speeches. His gift was being so prominent that nobody had the courage to tell him that his speeches were horrible.

In this chapter we are going to look at how to prepare a speech. Inadequate preparation is why most bad speeches fail. That is not to say that presentation is unimportant (we'll talk about that in the next chapter), but if you aren't willing to spend the time in preparation and do it properly, going before an audience will be as disastrous as jumping out of an airplane without a parachute.

> **A man has no ears for that to which experience has given him no access.**
>
> *Friedrich Wilhelm Nietzsche*

Consider the Audience

The first thing a speechwriter needs to consider is, strangely enough, the most neglected area in preparing a speech: the audience. Aside from the fact that time is the most precious gift an audience can give you and you should, consequently, not waste that gift, there are a number of other audience-related factors one should consider.

Some years ago, a man who was interested in proving a point about "art" put a paintbrush in a monkey's paw and taught the monkey to paint on a canvas. He then offered the monkey's work as his own. The "work of art" was quite abstract, colorful and modern, so the critics called it "interesting" and "unusual." Some of them even decided that the works were from the brush of one of the most important young artists of the day. The man never told the critics or those who bought the paintings about the monkey. After all, it was cheap labor and the monkey worked quickly.

A good speech, like good art, takes into account the fact that "self-expression" has no intrinsic value—it just *is*. A monkey can paint, and anybody can put words together. It is in the audience that something happens to make art great and speeches effective.

But, from that point on, the analogy begins to break down. Although art communicates, its communication is not necessarily cognitive. Art does not have the primary focus on an audience lest it cease to be art and become propaganda. But speech *must* focus on the audience, lest it become drivel. A speech must be concrete, clear in its message, and designed to elicit a response from those who hear it.

While there are some elements in preparing a speech that could be loosely described as an art form, I grow quite uncomfortable when rhetoric is described as "art." A speech isn't art. It is a tool, highly pragmatic, and aimed at a target: the audience.

Every once in a while some organization sponsors a contest to determine "the best sermons of the year." Preachers send in their sermons for evaluation, and a group of judges decides who wins the awards. Some of the best sermons ever preached would never win an award, get a good grade in a homiletics class, or be printed in a book of sermons. Do you know why? Because the judge, the only judge, of whether or not a sermon is good or bad is the audience.

A speech can't be judged by how beautiful, how organized, how graceful, or how refined it is. The only judge of a speech is the audience. I often tell my students, "Don't worry so much about your grade in here. If you show up, you will do okay. The real exam will be given when you actually go into the pulpit in your church. I am here, not to prepare you to make a good grade in this class, but to keep you from getting a failing mark in the exam that will be given by your congregations."

In preparing a speech, give great attention to your expected audience. The following questions should constitute a mental checklist through which you should go before preparing a speech or sermon:

What is the average age and gender of the audience?
What is the education of the audience?
Will the audience be hostile, supportive, or neutral?
Will the audience have to be convinced of the importance of the subject?
What will be the attention span of the audience?
What are the kinds of speeches to which this particular audience has in the past responded positively?

Let me give you a principle: In preparation, consideration of the audience precedes and defines form. In other words, the content and style of your speech will be dictated by the nature of the audience. Throughout the rest of this chapter I'm going to give you some help in preparing a speech. If you get all the rest right, and forget about the audience, your speech might be great "art" but not much else.

Consider the Subject

The second consideration in preparing a speech is the subject. Sometimes you will be assigned a topic. Sometimes you will be asked to focus on a certain general area. Other times your subject matter will be left entirely to your discretion. In the first instance, it is better to refuse to give the speech than it is to give one on a subject about which you know very little or for which your audience has no interest whatsoever. In the second instance, you will have to hone your speech according to your expertise and the level of audience interest. In the third instance, always accept the invitation!

Let me explain. . .

When a narrow topic is assigned, you must be very careful. Being able to "talk good" is not enough to cover your lack of knowledge or the audience's lack of interest. I am often asked to speak at conferences and colleges. Often the people who ask me assume, wrongly, that I can talk about anything that has to do with religion. After a lot of years on the speaking circuit, I have learned to say, "I'm sorry, but there are a lot of people who can handle that topic better than I can. If you can't give me a wider choice, you probably ought to get someone else."

When the subject is more general and loosely concerns your

> **What is the short meaning of the long speech?**
>
> *Johann von Schiller*

field of expertise, you have a fair amount of leeway. For instance, if the subject should be "How to Teach Children" and you are a parent, a schoolteacher, a Sunday school teacher, or a Little League baseball coach, you can accept the invitation, knowing that your speech will concentrate on that area of "teaching children" about which you know the most.

The best speaking invitations are those that give a wide berth as to subject matter. You get to go through your mind and play "smorgasbord" with subjects you find interesting and about which you can communicate best.

However, the problem with allowing you to choose your subject is to know which one to pick. There are three rules:

1. Pick a subject that will hold your attention.
2. Pick a subject that will hold the audience's attention.
3. Pick a subject about which you know something or, with research, can learn enough to make sense.

Whether your subject has been assigned or is one you have picked, you have the task of gathering material. I believe that you should at least start by collecting all the material you can find on the topic and making notes on anything that might possibly be included in the speech you are planning to give. Make note of all illustrations, statistical data, and facts regarding the subject.

At this point, don't try to organize anything. Just take notes until you have gathered all the material you can possibly use. It is a good practice to read the shortest published work you can find on your subject. It gives you an idea of what you are digging for.

The truth is that you will only use a small part of the material you collect in this first step of taking notes. However, even what you don't use in your speech will become a part of your "safety net" when you are delivering a speech. It is always wise to be prepared to speak from the overflow, but a speech should never contain everything you know on the subject.

When making a speech, especially if you do it often, you will find that much of the material you had not planned to use will come to mind while you are talking. It will even organize itself and come out properly. That is the function of the "librarian of your mind," who is constantly checking on words, facts, and stories. If there in nothing in the "stacks," the librarian won't be able to help you make a better speech.

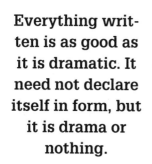

Everything written is as good as it is dramatic. It need not declare itself in form, but it is drama or nothing.

Robert Frost

Use the Funnel Principle

The next step in the preparation of a speech uses the "funnel principle." Here is where you start putting all your material through a funnel so that it will focus on specific ideas. This is a process of elimination. For instance, if your speech is about "How to Teach Children," you might have five or six pages of notes, detailing everything from how many children are in the public school system in America to the pedagogical theories of some top educators. You might have taken some notes on child psychology or on the difference between private education and public education. You may have found a lot of material on new methodologies of teaching or about experimental schools. Perhaps you have taken some notes on parental involvement in education or home-schooling. There might be some facts on "school choice" or extended school years. You might have found material on the bias in public education.

It is obvious that you can't cover all those topics or even work most of them into your speech because the mind won't absorb what the seat can't endure. So you have to start eliminating and organizing—the funneling process. It is where you focus on what will be included and excluded in your speech.

A good practice for me has been to make note, as I am taking notes from a variety of areas, of those particular points which interest or excite me. I call these the communication "points of light." As you go through your notes, some things will almost "jump off the page," shouting to you, "Use me! Use me!" I have found that it is good to trust your instincts at this point, always keeping in mind the audience and your own interest.

Now you can begin the process of organization. I usually take a piece of paper and list the "teaching points," those points that I want to communicate to my audience. I then combine as many points as possible, create main headings and subheadings, and develop an outline.

At the end of the funneling process, you ought to be able to say in a sentence or two what you are trying to accomplish in your speech. If that can't be done, then you need to go back and begin again to focus on the subject matter until you can articulate very quickly and very clearly the purpose and major theme of the speech.

Once again using the example of "How to Teach Children," let's say that you have funneled the subject down to one area which is school choice. Perhaps you have decided that school choice is a good idea. When you have "funneled," you ought to be able to say something like this: "In this speech, I intend to show my audience that, contrary to the position of many professional educators, school choice is good for children, for parents, and for America." (On the other hand, perhaps you want to show that school choice is a bad idea for children, parents, and the nation.)

Establish the Form

Now, you are ready to establish the form of your speech. There are three main elements: an introduction, the body of the speech, and the conclusion. Let's talk about each one of those parts of a speech.

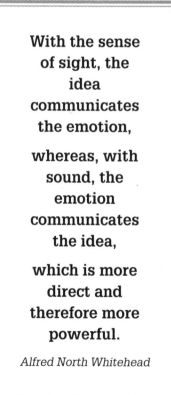

With the sense of sight, the idea communicates the emotion,

whereas, with sound, the emotion communicates the idea,

which is more direct and therefore more powerful.

Alfred North Whitehead

The Introduction

This is perhaps the most important part of a speech. Within the first minute of your speech, your audience is going to make a judgment about you and about whether or not they are interested in hearing anything else you have to say. Let me give you three "don'ts" and three "do's."

Don't apologize. More speeches have been hurt than you would believe by speakers who opened their speech with "I'm not much of a speaker . . ." or "I hope you will forgive my lack of preparation in this subject . . . " or "I didn't want to do this, and I'm very nervous . . . "

Don't demean. Your audience is giving you their time. They don't owe you anything. You owe them. When you make fun of the audience or become caustic or angry in your introduction, you might as well sit down. A song leader, in a poor attempt at humor, gave me the audience with these words: "Steve, this is a hard bunch, but I'm sure you will survive." When I got up to speak, it took me five precious minutes to get the audience back on my side.

Don't patronize. Speakers who show arrogance in their opening statements will die before they get to the body of the speech. There are some speakers who give the impression that they are preparing to speak from Sinai. There are also introductions that make the speaker feel as if he or she were going to speak from Sinai. You might think, "If I'm that good, I can hardly wait to hear what I have to say," but if you communicate that kind of attitude, you will have already lost the audience.

Lest you think that I am only giving negatives, here are three "do's."

Do get the audience's attention. There are lots of ways you can do this in an introduction to a speech. Continuing with the example of a speech on "How to Teach Children," you could make a startling statement of purpose: "I'm going to show you something today that will break your heart [shatter your illusions, bring tears to your eyes, etc.]." You could also get attention with an astounding fact: "Did you know that over 50 percent of the children in our public school system can't identify the last three presidents of the United States?" You might use humor: "Did you hear about the three boys who were in a huddle in the back of a room? The teacher asked them what they were doing, and they admitted that they were telling dirty jokes. The teacher said, "Thank goodness! I thought you were praying." Sometimes you can get an audience's attention by a well-placed compliment: "I have been looking forward to being here this evening because you have shown yourself to be concerned and intelligent citizens of our community."

Do whet the audience's appetite. A good opening will give your audience a desire to hear what is going to be said in the speech itself. If an audience doesn't have a vested interest in what you are about to say, the odds are that they won't pay attention. If you are giving a speech to death-row inmates on how to "beat the system," you are going to have an attentive audience. If you are going to speak about investments to entrepreneurs, they will listen. If you are going to deal with how to raise children, frustrated parents are going to listen to your every word. But let them know what's coming.

To follow through with the example of giving a speech on "How to Teach Children," you might begin, "The future of our nation is dependent on the education of our children. If we fail there, we fail as a nation." Or you could say, "W. C. Fields said that anybody who didn't like children or dogs couldn't be all bad. Jesus said to let the children come to him. Fields is dead and, for the most part, forgotten. Jesus is still the expert to whom people listen. Concern for children is the measure of a nation and an individual." You might ask a question: "Have you ever wondered why, despite the billions of dollars we spend on education in America, we have one of the poorest educational systems in the industrialized world?"

Do give the audience your theme. Someone has said that in a good speech a speaker will first tell the audience what he or she is going to say, then say it, and then conclude by telling them what was said. That is too simple, but there is a point to be made. It is important that the audience know the direction in which you are heading. If you wait until the end to state your purpose, it will be too late.

That is not to say that you should give away everything you are going to say. If that were the case, there would be no need for your speech. However, your theme or purpose ought to be stated, preferably in an arresting way. For instance: "I intend in the few moments we have together to show you how, when given a choice of schools, children who want to learn can make astounding educational progress. Further, I intend to show you that there are great numbers of people in our country who, for very selfish and ill-advised reasons would have you remain unaware of what I am going to say." (If, of course, you were taking the other side of the issue you might say, "During our time together, I plan to show you that there are some very narrow and biased folks who are trying to destroy the greatest institution in America, public education.")

Body of the Speech

Now, to the second part of a speech, its body, or substance. This is the place where you will communicate your main ideas, present your data, and make your case. There are two important principles to remember in preparing the body of your speech.

Principle #1. Your speech will be successful in direct proportion to how many of your audience's questions are anticipated and answered. The next time you are listening to a speech or sermon (assuming that you keep listening after the introduction), note how you react to what the speaker says. If you disagree with something, you will say in your mind, "That is nonsense!" If you are in strong agreement, you might whisper, "YESSSSSSS!" If the speaker is confusing, you will find yourself thinking, "I wish he would explain that a bit more. That seems to contradict what he said before." A speech is a dialogue between a speaker and an audience. One side of the dialogue is silent—but real. If you forget that, your speech will bomb.

Speakers with years of experience have learned to read an audience in terms of confusion, anger, or affirmation. However, if you are relatively new at this, you must anticipate the reaction by asking yourself questions: If I were in the audience, what would I want to know about this subject? What kind of questions would I ask? What will elicit a proper response?

Principle #2. There is also a direct correlation between the audience's ability to take notes and the effectiveness of your speech.

Please note that I did not say that an audience must take notes for your speech to be a success. However, if anyone in the audience wanted to take notes and could not do so because of your sloppy transitions, merging of points, and lack of clarity, your speech will be a failure.

I find it wise to number my points and as I move to the next point, I review points already made.

Watch transitions. They need to be clearly delineated and stated so that the audience can take notes, if they should so desire.

The Conclusion

The final part of a speech is not the place where you try to do what you failed to do so far. The conclusion should never be a time of review, unless the review can be made to "sizzle." Neither is it the time to try to recover what you have already lost or to make another point.

The conclusion of a speech is the time to end with a bang. There is nothing worse than a speech that was making it up to the conclusion but dies at the end.

There is cognitive communication where the object is to communicate a definable message of facts, points, and conclusions. And then there is emotive communication which is primarily designed to solicit emotion. The conclusion of a speech should, of course, have an element of the cognitive—but it is terribly important that it also be primarily emotive. A good story can be emotive. A pithy line can be emotive, as can humor. However you do it, make sure that there is some strong emotive stuff in your conclusion. A speech without an emotive conclusion is like a rocket that dies on the launching pad.

For instance, following through with our speech idea of teaching children, a conclusion might be as follows:

> This evening we have taken the time to think of our children's future. When we discuss educational choice, we must look beyond the politics, the economics, and the vested interest of educators. We must remember the children.
>
> Socrates once said, "Could I climb to the highest place in Athens, I would lift my voice and proclaim: 'Fellow citizens, why do ye turn and scrape every stone to gather wealth, and take so little care of your children, to whom one day you must relinquish it all?'"

Let me give you three rules about conclusions:

1. A conclusion must be short. There is nothing worse than speakers who, having said all that they came to say, keep on talking.

2. A conclusion needs to be conclusive. Have you ever listened to a reasonably good speech and thought that there were three or four times at which the speaker would have done well to conclude? Make your conclusion a formal and clearly definable part of your speech.

3. If your speech has bombed before the conclusion, the conclusion probably won't save it. But it might. So, go with it anyway. Sometimes a very bad speech is saved by a very good conclusion. (Not a bad line, I thought, with which to *conclude* this chapter.)

9

How to Give a Speech

He taught them as one having authority,
and not as the scribes.
Matt. 7:29

Let's talk about actually giving a speech.

Perhaps you, like a lot of others, are saying, "I would rather go to the dentist, face an IRS audit, and confront my wife's ex-husband than give a speech. My mouth goes dry, my palms sweat, and my hands start shaking at just the thought of giving a speech."

If giving a speech is your second least favorite thing in the world, right after jumping off buildings, and if the thought of giving a speech leaves you speechless—great!

Nobody ever gave a *good* speech without being afraid. That fear, when channeled properly, will be the very thing that will create an effective speech.

My friend John DeBrine, host of the radio program "Songtime," believes in a doctrine called Dying Grace. He believes that when it is a Christian's time to die, God will give special grace so that the death itself will be far easier

than the thought of dying. He believes that Christians who
face death will be given great peace and that the "home
going" will be a joyful occasion.

I once visited John just before he was to undergo major
surgery. I asked him if he was afraid. He said, "I'm scared
to death, and if I wasn't scared, I would be really scared."

Giving a speech is sort
of like that. If you aren't
afraid, you ought to be.
If there isn't a significant
amount of anxiety, you
are probably going to
give a lousy speech. The
fact is, most experienced
speakers feel a great deal
of anxiety before they
speak. I have given literally thousands of ser-
mons and speeches, but
I have never been before
an audience or a congre-
gation that I didn't want
to run from.

> The best way to
> make an
> impression is by
> making the
> impression that
> you're not trying
> to make an
> impression.
>
> *George Hart*

So, before we get into
the actual methodolo-
gies of giving a speech, let me say a word about fear. That
word is **LEVEL**. It is an acrostic. If you remember it and practice it, you can deal with your fear.

Legitimize Your Fear

The only people who say they aren't afraid of making a
speech are liars and fools. Speaking before an audience is
an anxiety-producing experience. Anyone who doesn't feel
a certain amount of anxiety before speaking simply doesn't
understand the situation.

During my radio station days I once interviewed a buyer for a large department store in Boston. The store was one of the station's major clients and a part of the advertising contract included an interview. Because I wanted to make this young woman feel comfortable, I said to her, "Don't let the microphone intimidate you. You and I will just be talking, and the microphone is incidental to that."

"Don't worry," she said, "This is easy, and I can assure you that the microphone doesn't bother me. This is what I do for a living."

"Okay," I said, turning on the recorder. "I have with me today one of the buyers at ———, and we are going to be talking about the new fall line of women's clothes. Tell me, Sara, what is hot and what is not?"

Silence.

Thinking that she had not heard or understood the question, I repeated it. Once again there was silence, so I turned off the recorder. I noticed tears welling up in her eyes. "I guess," she said, "I was more nervous than I thought."

Yes, she was. It would have been far better for her to face the reality of her fear and talk it out with me, than to deny her fear and have it—like a snake in the grass—sneak up on her and bite her.

One time a farmer was plowing and there was a horse-fly on the rear of the donkey pulling the plow. His son reached over and flipped the horsefly away. The farmer said, "Why did you do that? It was the only thing that made him go."

Fear is a wonderful "motivator." It can put you on the cutting edge of giving a speech. It sharpens your mind and it creates in you the potential of being at your best. If you don't have anxiety about a speech, it is probably going to bomb.

Now, *that* ought to scare you.

Elucidate Your Fear

As we saw in the second chapter of this book, demons die in the light. It is important, when you are dealing with fear, to think about your fear and then name the reasons you are afraid.

When I was a pastor, I once visited a woman in the hospital who was facing major surgery the next day. I asked her if she was afraid. Most of the time, if I asked Christians whether they were afraid they gave me the answer they thought I expected: "No, Pastor. God is faithful, and through His help I am dealing with my fear."

Not this woman. When I asked her if she was afraid, she said, "Are you crazy? Of course I'm afraid! This is a hospital. People die in hospitals!"

I loved her answer. Do you know why? Because not only was she afraid, she knew why she was afraid.

Just so, learn to name your fears about speechmaking. When you name them you can deal with them. Are you afraid that people will think you made a fool of yourself? Are you afraid that people won't understand the importance of the subject of your speech? Are you afraid that people will discover the truth about you? Are you afraid that you will antagonize your friends? Are you afraid of being alone? Are you afraid that you will lose your job? Are you afraid that, if you bomb, you won't get the expected promotion? Are you afraid because you have a bad self-image? Are you afraid because you are a "people pleaser" and don't want to disappoint anyone?

Whatever your fear, learn to name it.

But don't stop there. Ask yourself what would be the worst thing that could happen if your fears were realized. If you lost your job, would you be able to get another one? (Of course you would.) If you don't get the promotion, would there be other opportunities? (Of course there would. You would just have to work a little harder.) Will people really reject you because of one speech? (Maybe. But if they did, you don't want to be associated with anyone that superficial anyway.)

The point is this: You must demythologize your fears. Fear is a horrible thing when you allow it to go unchecked, undefined, and unchallenged.

Visualize Your Success

I mentioned this in chapter 2, but let me emphasize the point in particular of thinking about giving a speech. Do you remember the words about fear in Shakespeare's *Julius Caesar*? (If you don't, you were taught by a "politically correct" teacher who was a "twit.") Caesar says, "Cowards die many times before their deaths; the valiant never taste of death but once." (Act II, Sc. 2, Line 32)

Cowards die a thousand deaths because they are constantly visualizing their dying. It is the same way with speeches. If you persist in visualizing your speech bombing, even if it does you will have gone through the experience a number of times. Instead, visualize your speech being a tremendous success.

I spend a great portion of my time on airplanes and I hate them. In fact, I have yet to put all of my weight on one jet. But I have a friend who loves flying. I asked him if he didn't sometimes think about the airplane crashing. "Oh, yes," he replied. "I picture myself helping people who are hurt and working with the rescue squad to save lives."

It dawned on me that his visualization of an airplane crash and mine were quite different. He saw, in his mind's eye, himself unhurt and helping others while I saw, in my mind's eye, myself as among the injured. That was the difference between his courage and my fear.

It is the same way with a speech. Instead of concentrating on what could go wrong, concentrate on what could go right. Visualize yourself as speaking clearly, moving the audience with the power of your words, and accepting (of course, with great humility) the praise of those who heard the speech. It is amazing what a change in mind pictures can do with fear.

Embrace Your Fear

Fear tends to increase in direct proportion to how much you run from it. People always say to me when they hear of my fear of flying, "Steve, you are a Christian. You shouldn't be afraid to fly."

"If I weren't a Christian," I always reply, "I wouldn't even get near an airplane. If I go down, I will always go up. That thought gives me enough courage to get on the plane and sit there until they lock the door and we are in the air. Then it is too late to run."

But the truth is, I know that if I ever run from getting on a plane, I'll never get on one again. It is only in facing my fear, doing what I fear and surviving, that I am able to deal with it.

It is the same with making a speech. If the night before the speech you call up the organizer of the event and plead sickness or death or jungle rot, you will never give a speech again. The worst part is that you will always know that you "copped out" of something that you should have done. Remember the English proverb I gave you in the second chapter? "Fear knocked on the door; faith answered and nobody was there."

If you are afraid, that is normal. It's okay. If you think that your whole world is going to come falling down because of what you think will be a horrible speech, that is understandable. If your knees are knocking and your mouth is dry, it's all right. But it is not okay or understandable or all right to not give the speech. Do it! Do it! You will be surprised at how easy it is, once you get going.

Liberate Yourself

When I say that you should "liberate yourself," I mean that you should talk to yourself and become your most enthusiastic cheerleader. The best speakers are always giving themselves pep talks.

Did you hear about the man who was in the supermarket with his two-year-old son? The little boy kept pulling down from the shelves everything he could get his hands on. The father would replace the item and would say, "Calm yourself, Ronnie." The boy would run off and hit the other customers, and the father would say, "Calm yourself, Ronnie." When they were going through the checkout line, the little boy toppled a whole candy display, and the father said, "Calm yourself, Ronnie."

Finally, one of the customers, having taken as much as she could stand, said to the father, "Sir, your little boy is a hellion. He needs a good swift kick in the pants, and all you can say is 'Calm yourself, Ronnie.'"

"Madam," the father answered, "you don't understand. My boy's name is Mike. I'm Ronnie!"

I suspect that the father should have done more than talk to himself, but he should have, at least, done that. You should do that too.

Lillian Glass, in her book, *Say It Right*, says,

Communication involves three things: It reflects how we feel about ourselves, how it affects others, and it is a means by which we are affected by others. Awareness of these three aspects of communication can enhance your ability as a good communicator . . . Even though you've had years of negative conditioning, you can change. You can retrain your inner voice to talk positively—to say encouraging things to yourself and not beat yourself up when you make a mistake. A side benefit to doing this is that oftentimes your vocal tone

will improve as you become more confident. (New York:
The Putnam Publishing Group, 1992, pp. 67-68)

She makes a very good point. Learn to cheer yourself up. Learn to say, "I'm just as good as anyone in this audience." Learn to give yourself permission to be human. Learn to be your own best cheerleader, and you will be surprised at the difference it will make with your fear of speaking.

That is the way to LEVEL your fear. Use these principles, along with the material in the second chapter of this book. Then you'll be well on the way to dealing with the fear of making a speech.

Now, let's turn to the actual delivery of a speech. One of the problems is that books on speech give you so much to remember that, after reading them, most people don't remember any of it. It is possible to suffer from the problem of "cognitive glut" and find yourself failing to give an effective speech, not because you don't know enough, but because you know too much.

> **A bishop . . . asked David Garrick, the great actor, how it was possible to take fiction and produce such a tremendous effect on his audience. Garrick replied, "Because I recite fiction as if it were truth, and you preach truth as if it were fiction."**
>
> *Walter L. Lingle*

The Ten Commandements of Giving a Speech

There are entire books written on the art of making a speech—but you don't have to read them. I'm going to give you ten points that, if you remember and practice them, they will go a long way to making you a successful and even gifted speaker. (Of course, in chapter 7, I gave you five rules. That makes fifteen in all. Maybe I've gone too far too.)

I call these rules, "The Ten Commandments" of standing before an audience and giving a speech. Listen up! What follows is important.

The First Commandment
Thou Shalt Not Be Unprepared

By this I don't mean to reiterate what I said in chapter 8 about preparing a speech. Here I am talking about becoming familiar with the content of your speech.

There are some who recommend memorizing a speech. That is fine if you are usually "cool under fire." The problem with memorizing a speech and acquiring the reputation of speaking without notes, is that nervousness can make it easy to forget what you have memorized. And the second mistake (total blackout) is greater than the first (memorizing).

When I was a pastor, some couples memorized the vows they would be making during their marriage ceremony. Most of them blew it, because they didn't realize how nervous they would be during the actual ceremony. Fortunately, I always had them give me a copy of the vows so I could prompt them when they forgot their lines.

When you give a speech, you won't have anybody to prompt you, so it is best to bring along some notes (maybe an entire manuscript). If you get into trouble (e.g., suddenly find that your lipstick is smeared or your zipper is down), you can always lean on your notes.

But, with all that being said, you ought to be so familiar with your material that you are not dependent on your notes or your manuscript. By going over your speech in your mind—making sure you are familiar with the main points, the illustrations, the introduction, and the conclusion—you will be free to concentrate on your topic and, especially, on the audience.

Now a word about reading a manuscript. It is okay to read a speech as long as it isn't too obvious that you are doing so. The only way you can acquire the ability to read a speech as if you weren't reading it, is to make sure that this first commandment is obeyed. Eye contact is very important in making a speech. When reading, there is the danger of losing eye contact with your audience. Read if you must, but don't speak like you are reading.

The Second Commandment
Thou Shalt Not Have One Method of Giving a Speech

Just as there are "different strokes for different folks," there are different methodologies for giving a speech. I had a pastor friend who was so against the Vietnam War that almost all his sermons during that period concerned why we should not be in Vietnam. I said to him one time, "Sam, when this war is over, you aren't going to have anything to say." He didn't appreciate my comments, especially when I added, "I'll be glad when this thing is over for a lot of reasons, but one of them is that you are going to have to stick to religion in your sermons."

Just as my friend had only one theme, some speakers have one technique. For instance, you can't speak to an audience of ten in the same way you speak to an audience of a thousand. When the audience consists of ten people, it is wise to be informal, casual, and conversational. When speaking to an audience of a thousand, you must project, make your gestures broader, and become more formal.

After you have spoken often before an audience, you will find that you are far more at ease (not without fear) than you were when you gave your first speech. At that point, it is wise to learn to speak extemporaneously (dealing with a subject without notes) or to hone your skills at watching an audience and reacting to their visual cues. This, of course, is not for beginners, but, as you speak more often, you will learn to gear your style to your audience.

For instance, you don't speak to teenagers in the same way you would to college professors. A ladies aid social requires something quite different from the local chapter of Alcoholics Anonymous. One methodology of speaking is needed for talking to your little boy's kindergarten class and a totally different one is used when addressing the graduates of West Point.

Be careful to fit your methodology to your audience.

The Third Commandment
Thou Shalt Not Concentrate on Thyself

A certain amount of self-awareness is required in a good speaker. However, if you are totally concentrated on yourself, you will miss the whole reason for your speech: communicating something important to an audience.

I never gave sex manuals to couples who came to me for premarital counseling. Do you know why? (No, that's not the reason.) Because I figured that, as my friend Harold Myra says in his wonderful little book, *Is There A Place I Can Scream?* (London: Hodder and Stoughton, 1975, pp. 39-40), it is rather natural.

Thanks, Lord,
thanks for our sexuality
For the whole marvellous idea of our male/femaleness.

Why make sex so powerful, Lord,
like a twenty-pound gland in a hundred-pound body?

Did you mis-engineer, Lord?
Or are we misdirected gluttons?

It's got to be powerful, sure
to keep the species going.
But if you'd toned it down a little, Lord,
I'm sure I'd still get around to my part.

Sex, like talking, is normal. (Of course, although sexual
intimacy is always natural, it is moral only within the context of marriage.) Just as we are sexual beings, we are also
beings who communicate with one another. You don't have
to think hard about talking—you just have to talk. You
don't need to concentrate on talking—you just open your
mouth and communicate what is on your mind. Most of
us do quite well with communication within our regular
day-to-day relationships, and there is no reason to assume
that (unless you work hard at it) you will do so terribly
when you stand before an audience.

To change the metaphor, giving a speech is like driving
a car, riding a bicycle, or swimming. The more you do it,
the less you think about it. It becomes second nature.
Because communicating with other human beings is a natural function, much of the art of speaking before an audience involves eliminating the fear of speaking before an
audience. The Bible and a good speech book will give you
the same advice: Don't think so much about yourself—
think about them.

The Fourth Commandment
Thou Shalt Not Make Long Speeches

This commandment requires very little elaboration, so I
will keep it short, the way you ought to keep your speeches.
The longer the speech, the greater the chance of failure.

The Fifth Commandment
Thou Shalt Not Listen to Everyone's Criticism

If you ask people what they think of your speech, either before you give it or after it is over, they are going to tell you. The problem here is that most people, even good speakers, are not good critics. They have a tendency to universalize their own private feeling. That can sometimes be helpful, but it can also be dangerous since the private feeling of one person may not reflect what will be (or was) the reaction of the audience.

I have a deep voice (this is one of the obvious assets of which I cannot be proud, given the fact that I was born with it), and what I say to people who don't know me has a tendency to intimidate them or sound bombastic. Even when I am trying to be quite humble, I sound like I'm speaking with authority.

One time as a man who came to me for counseling was leaving my office, he mentioned that he was going to see his doctor about a medical problem. I told him not to worry. "Lots of people have that problem, and most of them find out that it isn't serious. In fact, the test will be quite simple and quick. If the problem requires hospitalization, it will only be for a day or two."

The man left my office feeling really good. But the advice I gave him was wrong. My secretary at the time said, "Steve, you must be careful about giving medical advice. People believe you, and you don't know what you are talking about!"

Some critiques of speeches are like my comments on medical problems: without understanding or knowledge.

Let me suggest that you find someone you trust and, more particularly, someone who knows something about the art of rhetoric. Ask that person to give you honest criticism. It will be worth the comments of a thousand others.

One other thing: Family members are usually not the best critics of your speeches. At any point in your relationship with them, they will either love you or be ticked at you. Love and anger can warp criticism.

The Sixth Commandment
Thou Shalt Not Mumble

Speaking clearly is a prerequisite for an audience hearing clearly. (Now, that's a profound statement!) By that I mean to suggest that you should work on your speech pattern. In teaching seminary students in communication classes, I have found that most of them are not even aware of how they sound. They think they are doing fine, and up to that point nobody has had the courage to say, "You talk so fast no one can understand a thing you say." "You have a habit of blurring your words when you are nervous." "You don't project. No one heard you beyond the third row." "You mispronounce most words of over two syllables." "You have a terrible nasal whine."

Elocution is important to you because it is important to your audience. Ask a trusted acquaintance about your speech habits who will tell you the truth about your delivery. Listen to yourself on tape, and learn, thereby, to be your own best critic. When you are going through the "postmortem" of a speech, be honest with yourself about the areas where there needs to be improvement.

One time my brother Ron was asked to say grace before a meal. He mumbled something that could loosely be classified as a prayer. Our mother said, "Ron, I didn't hear you."

"Mother," Ron said, "I wasn't talking to you."

I suspect that God can understand mumbling, but God already knows what you are going to say before you say it. The audience, unfortunately, doesn't have that advantage.

The Seventh Commandment
Thou Shalt Be Thyself

Most good speakers, at one time or another, copy the style of their favorite and most respected oratory heroes.

As a matter of fact, I think this is a good practice when you first begin to speak publicly. But that copy must have personal elements to it, it must be geared to one's own style and gifts, and it must not clearly be an imitation. In that case, people will ignore what you say and go to hear the genuine article.

There are those who still say to me, "Steve, do you know that you sound a little like John DeBrine?" There is a reason for that. When I first started speaking, John DeBrine was my mentor. I was a disc jockey in Boston, and John was a Baptist preacher. For some reason, he took an interest in me. I spent a lot of time with John at the beach or driving with him to one of his speaking engagements. For years I would listen to him preach and would say to myself, "If I could only communicate that way, I could change the world."

Although it is no accident that I sound a little like John DeBrine in my communicating style, only those who know both John and me quite well can tell. I have, over the years, developed my own style and methodology, but I will always be grateful to John for providing the "scaffolding" in those early years.

But the nature of scaffolding is that it is meant to be removed after the building is complete. It is the same way with one who copies the style of another speaker. It is okay to do some of that at the beginning, but a speaker ought to very quickly develop his or her own style and methods.

Phillips Brooks, the famous rector of Trinity Church in Boston, said, "Preaching is truth through personality." That is a good definition of preaching, and with slight modification could become a good definition of speaking. Speaking ought to be truth through personality. (I suppose that a liar could develop into an effective speaker. Politicians do it all the time. However, that ought not to be the goal of a speaker—certainly not an ethical one.)

There is only one of you. God made you unique. It is a sin to take an original and try to copy it.

One of the reasons I don't require my students to fit into a "mold" of what a good preacher should be is that each of them is different. What works for one, won't work for another. My goal in teaching young people to communicate publicly is to help them be the best they can within their own style and gifts. It ought to be the goal you set for yourself too.

The Eighth Commandment
Thou Shalt Speak Gently

We live in a new age where old ways are ineffective. One of the problems with many preachers is that they preach the way Jonathan Edwards preached. Now, the message ought to be the same, but Jonathan Edwards lived in a time when there was no television. He dealt with an audience whose main entertainment was listening to a sermon, and the most exciting thing to happen during any week was the new line of feed at the general store. Every speech, from political speeches to Fourth of July orations, was modeled after the sermon.

While I'm not big on the entertainment value of sermons, I would like to go back to a slower time when "grass" was something you mowed, not smoked; where being "gay" was a positive personality trait, not a sexual lifestyle; where "Coke" was something you got from a soda fountain, not a drug dealer; and where AIDS was what one did for others instead of an abbreviation for a disease. I really don't like all the changes, but how one person feels about it doesn't matter. My feelings are irrelevant. What is, just is. If I am to be an effective communicator, I must be aware of the changes.

Ours is an anti-authoritarian era. The more you insist on your importance, the less important you will be. In an age of "cool" communication, the louder you yell, the less people will listen. Savvy communicators will not pontificate, they will discuss and reason.

That is all to say that the "shout" is "out." That doesn't mean that there won't be an occasional shout in a speech to get attention—but the shout will be controlled, focused, and limited. It is not to say that emotion should not be a part of a good speech, but that uncontrolled emotion tends to cause a negative emotional reaction to your speech.

It is my hope that in our time of great social change, shouting will once again be "in," that pounding a lectern will once again be an effective communicating technique. Then I will be able to plead with great emotion, for I'm good at all those things. But, for now, wise communicators will turn down the volume. They should communicate "Can we talk?" rather than "This is the law and you will obey."

The Ninth Commandment
Thou Shalt Watch Body Language

This is not a book on body language. But in communication body language is almost as important as the words you speak.

A number of years ago, I discovered that my counseling technique left something to be desired. People would come to me already intimidated by the fact that I was a clergyman. Combining that with my foghorn voice and my naturally intense style, made counseling time in my study seem like the equivalent of a visit with a harsh stepfather, rather than a visit with someone who wanted to help.

A friend told me, "Steve, you can't change your voice, you can't stop being a pastor, but you can change your body language. Instead of leaning forward to listen intently to what the person is saying, lean back in your chair. Don't cross your arms as if you were a Buddha waiting to deliver a message. Keep your posture open and nonthreatening. Get out from behind your desk and sit in an easy chair."

The change was amazing. People started talking instead of confessing. People left my office feeling helped rather than condemned and the change in my body language relaxed even me. (Remember the principle? If you act in a certain way, the role may become the reality.)

The same idea applies to public speaking. You should be erect but not rigid. Don't always stand behind a lectern (or use the pulpit); it is a symbolic barrier to good communication. Develop friendly body language (palms open and reaching toward the audience), rather than authoritarian gestures (the rabbit chop or arms crossed over the chest). Make sure there is good eye contact. When you don't look at your audience, they will think you are lying. Learn to smile every once in a while. When you do, the audience will smile back.

Sometimes, of course, there are occasions when a sermon or a speech needs to be authoritarian. When that happens, reverse everything I said in the last paragraph.

The Tenth Commandment
Thou Shalt Deviate

Variety is the spice of life and the stuff of a good speech. Speakers can get into speech patterns that need to be broken. My friend Ben Haden, one of the finest communicators in America, has mastered the technique of the "pregnant pause." He has the ability to just stop occasionally and wait until everyone is leaning forward to hear what he is going to say. (Someone said that I could give an entire sermon in one of Ben's pauses.) Zig Ziglar is a rapid-fire speaker. Ben will speed up the pace and Zig will slow it down to get attention.

> **Criminologists claim few acts of violence are committed after a hearty meal. This prolongs the life of speakers.**
>
> *Pic Larmour*

The point is simply this: Anything, even if it is good, can go stale. If you are a quiet, reasoned talker, learn to raise your voice a bit occasionally. Sometimes, not often, you need to shout. If you are a facts-oriented speaker, you need to tell an emotional story once in a while. If you have a tendency to rely on emotive communication, quote a dull statistic every once in a while.

Keep an audience guessing and you will keep them awake. Give them what they expect in style and in content, and they will not bother to listen.

Now take the ten commandments of making a speech and rehearse them over and over again.

Before Billy Graham preached before great crowds in huge stadiums, he was a student who preached to the birds and the lizards in the woods of Florida. I don't know if the birds and the lizards were converted, but they could not have helped but be impressed.

A rule of thumb is this: Before anyone ever hears your speech, *you* should have heard it at least ten times. If you can find some attentive birds and lizards, that's okay too.

10

Keeping the "Bombs" from Exploding

If you have been foolish in exalting yourself,
or if you have devised evil,
put your hand on your mouth.
Prov. 30:32

If you are ever going to be proficient in communicating to others, whether in conversation, debate, or giving a speech, you must take risks. If you risk, you will sometimes fail. That is a fact.

Sometimes, if you risk, your conversation will be disjointed and you will feel ill at ease. Sometimes you will get bloodied in debate, and sometimes your audience will be gone before your speech ends.

If you aren't willing to risk failing, don't try. You see, there is no way to get from here to there without some significant bombs. In this chapter I'll show you how to keep those bombs from exploding.

Before we turn to how one handles a communication failure, I want to take a moment to say something about how you should handle success in communication. (I believe it is easier to handle failure than it is to handle success.)

It was a very wise preacher who said to a parishioner, after an extravagant and positive comment on his sermon, "You didn't need to tell me that. The devil beat you to it!"

Rating Effective Communication

Let me give you five ideas to consider when you know you have communicated effectively, been a wonderful conversationalist, won a debate, or given an incredibly great speech.

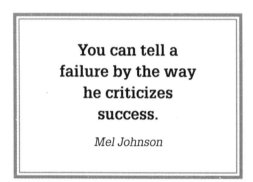

You can tell a failure by the way he criticizes success.

Mel Johnson

1. Remember how fleeting success really is. One time Napoleon was being greeted by great crowds shouting his praises as he returned from a successful battle where his victory had been complete. A close lieutenant remarked that it must be wonderful to receive so much praise from so many people. Napoleon said, "Nonsense! With a slightly different set of circumstances, this same crowd would be shouting for my death on the gallows."

It is a human proclivity to think that when you are successful you will always be successful and that when you have failed, you will always fail. Neither is true. In the latter case, that should be a point of encouragement and in the former, it should be motivation for humility.

2. Remember that everything you have is the result of God's providence (if you are a believer) or luck (if you aren't). Only an idiot looks back and attributes his or her success to a singular ability to "make it happen." It could easily have happened in just the opposite way. Movie stars who are honest and successful will tell you that there are many others who had more talent and worked harder and yet were not successful. Any successful musician will tell you that there are other musicians who are better and unknown. Any speaker who is successful at it, will tell you that there are better speakers all over the place who get no recognition.

If you remember that, it will give you a spirit of thankfulness for your success. That is an important and winsome trait in every successful communicator.

3. *When you are successful, remember that you are probably not nearly as good as you think you are when you are hearing the applause of the audience.* A man had just given a speech at his town's Rotary Club and was quite pleased with himself. "I wonder," he said to his wife, "how many great speakers our little town has produced."

"I think," she replied, "that our town has produced one less than you think."

As I mentioned before, a number of years ago a study was done of top executives in the Fortune 500 companies. One of the recurring themes in the psychological makeup of those executives was a fear that someone might discover the truth: that they got where they were by accident. Wise and successful communicators will always realize that they aren't half as good as those who applaud are implying, and not half as bad as those who criticize might suggest.

After I wrote my first book, one of the men I most respected wrote a highly critical letter to me. He said that I wrote like a child and that he couldn't believe I would write something so superficial. I was so devastated by his remarks that I determined never to write again and told him so. "I appreciate your honesty," I wrote to him, "and I want you to know that I have decided that you are right.

I have already signed a contract for a second book. But, after that one is published, I will give my time and gifts to something I do better."

When my second book was published, I got another letter from the man. He told me that my second book was one of the finest he had read. He told me that I was the "new C. S. Lewis of America."

That was when the light came on. I realized that my first book was not as bad as he said—but I also realized that my second book was not as good as he said.

4. *When you are successful, don't complain about the price of that success.* Someone has said that if you work hard in your job for forty hours a week, your boss will notice and give you a promotion, and then you can work hard for sixty hours a week. If you are successful, it will require even harder work. Don't complain about it. If you are successful, people will expect more success. Don't complain about it. If you are successful, you will have to do far better the next time. Don't complain about it.

There is a price tag attached to success and sometimes it is a very high price. But you will be recognized and paid in dollars or praise. You will feel good about yourself, at least for a while, and you will find a number of doors open to you that were not open before.

So when the dues are due, pay them, and don't complain about it.

5. *Remember that it is harder to learn from success than it is to learn from failure.* My friend Fred Smith has a wonderful definition of old age. He says that throughout life, people struggle to reach a certain plateau. When they reach it, they rest awhile and then begin to climb to the next plateau. Fred says that when one walks in circles on the same plateau rather than climbing higher, that person is old.

That is also a good definition of a dead speaker who hasn't been buried yet. When you fail, it can be a wonderful motivation for climbing higher, struggling more, and achieving better results next time. There is nothing more boring than a retired athlete who is constantly referring to past glories—except a speaker who is still giving the same speech because it worked the first time.

Handling Failed Communication

Now let's turn to the real bombs. What do you do when you have failed? In other words, what do you do when you have talked so people won't listen?

Avoid These Behaviors

There are five "don'ts" that are important.

1. Don't forget the parking lot. When Ben Haden was a young pastor, he conducted a series of evangelistic services in the town where he had once worked as an editor for the local newspaper. Ben said that he did the best he could and, at the end of his sermon, gave an invitation for any to come forward if they wanted to see God change their lives. Nobody came forward.

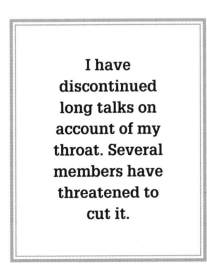

> I have discontinued long talks on account of my throat. Several members have threatened to cut it.

Ben was devastated until the pastor, noticing Ben's dejection, said to Ben, "Son, don't forget the one in the parking lot." Then he took Ben over to the window of the church overlooking the parking lot. There, on the gravel, was a man on his knees receiving Christ.

Even if you aren't a preacher, the illustration still works. If you have read and applied the principles in this book, your communication will at least be passable. If you have debated, engaged in conversation, or given a speech and think that it was a major failure, it may not have been as bad as you think.

I once spoke for a gathering of two thousand teenagers at a conference. Every time I think about that time, I blush. It was terrible. When it was over, I went backstage, called a cab, and left without anyone seeing me.

Some fifteen years later I was speaking at another conference when a young man came up to me and said, "Steve, you don't know me but about fifteen years ago, when I was a teenager, I was at a conference where you spoke. [I winced.] I just wanted to say thank you for what you said then. My life will never be the same because of that speech. Not only that, I taped what you said. Over the years, I have loaned that tape to a number of my friends. It has always touched them deeply."

How about that, sports fans?

Don't forget about the parking lot.

2. *Don't define yourself in terms of one failure.* It is said that when Demosthenes, the most famous of the Greek orators, gave his first speech, it was horrible. As he was walking away in shame from the hall, he heard someone say, "It wasn't a very good speech, but Demosthenes, at times, sounded a little like Pericles" (Athenian statesman of a previous generation).

That offhand compliment was the motivating factor which led Demosthenes to overcome his weak voice and delivery. He was the one who practiced speaking with pebbles in his mouth.

When I am listening to the first sermons of my students, I realize that I have a very great responsibility. One student said to me once, "Dr. Brown, I want you to be real hard on me. I can take it." I wanted to say, "Son, if you knew how bad you really are, you would never preach another sermon." I, of course, didn't say that. Do you know why? Because he sounded, at times, a little like Billy Graham.

Perhaps, after you have failed (or think you have), you won't have anyone to encourage you with a small compliment. But remember, nobody ever talks good who didn't, at first, talk bad. In other words, a poor speech or a lost debate should not be the measurement of lasting failure. Find someone who will say one good thing about your communication skills. Let that be the seed from which you create your next success.

3. *Don't let a negative mind-set create more failure.* For many years I said, "I never wanted to be a pastor. I am not a volunteer. I'm a conscript, and there are heel marks from where I was to where I am now."

One time my mentor said to me, "Steve, do you know the problem with saying things like that?" I allowed that I didn't. "It is a portable foxhole for you. If you fail, you can say, 'I never wanted to do this in the first place.'"

He was right. Because of a number of psychological issues in my life, I expected failure and prepared myself for it.

For a number of reasons, a lot of us expect failure. Because we expect it, we create it. Perhaps you are from a dysfunctional family or have been through a traumatic emotional experience. Or maybe you have been told so often that you would never amount to anything that you have come to believe it.

If that is true, an embarrassment in a conversation with a friend, a lost debate, or a speech that bombs is liable to ruin the rest of your life. Don't let it.

Let me give you one of the working principles of the universe. When a cat sits on a hot stove, the cat will never sit on a hot stove again—but it won't sit on a cold one either. It is possible to draw too much data from one lesson. If you failed, that means only that you failed, not that you are a failure. Don't let the demons of the past destroy your future.

4. Don't let your sense of theology (if you are a believer) create more failure. Some Christians have a strange proclivity to think they deserve failure. Someone has said that God is only a crutch. Well, of course He is! The question is not whether God is a crutch, but whether or not you have a limp. Wise people know about the universal limp, so they turn to God. That is as it ought to be. If you are a sinner, you need forgiveness. If you have been rejected, you need acceptance. If you are afraid, you need courage. If you are suicidal, you need a reason to live.

Those who know the truth, know that God is the only real and ultimate source of forgiveness, acceptance, courage, and meaning. But it is also important to remember that once you have been forgiven, you are forgiven. If you have been accepted, you are accepted. If you have been given courage, it will last. If you have found a meaning for your existence, you don't lose it.

Habit patterns die hard. There are a lot of people who act wisely in going to God, but they still live as if they had never been there. Nothing in the Bible suggests that God has some vested interest in pointing out your failures. God doesn't say, "Let's see if I can make Sam and Sara miserable." God is for you. Don't fail and then blame God for your failures. More importantly, don't keep on failing because you think God delights in failure.

5. Don't quit. Always remember that the only difference between successful people and failures is that the successful ones got up and tried again the last time they failed.

Life is a process, and Christians know that God is almost as interested in the direction of the process as in the final outcome. Learning to talk so people will listen is a process too. Don't expect to skip some steps of the process or

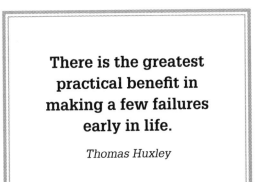

> **There is the greatest practical benefit in making a few failures early in life.**
>
> *Thomas Huxley*

try to be me. Whatever you do, don't truncate the process altogether. Get up from your failure and go at it again.

Practice These Behaviors

And now, before we finish, let me give you the four "do's" of failure.

1. Do analyze the failure. I have a friend who used to play football with the Miami Dolphins. He said that the worst part about being a professional football player was the post-mortem film. Each team has a film made of the game. During the week after the game the coach and players go over that film in great detail. My friend said that if he had made a mistake during a game, he had to watch a replay of that mistake over and over again until he found himself replaying it in his dreams. "But," he said, "I usually don't make the same mistake again."

After you have embarrassed yourself in a conversation, lost a debate, or given a horrible speech, don't just feel miserable. Any Bozo can do that. The difference between successful communicators and unsuccessful communicators is that the former don't just feel miserable, they analyze why they feel miserable.

Use this book as a measuring device and ask yourself which principles you violated. Talk to a trusted friend who will tell you the truth without destroying you. If possible, listen to a tape of your speech or debate and be honest with yourself about what you did wrong. Then list some ways that you can do it better the next time.

2. Do own the failure. One of the greatest hindrances to emotional healing is what psychologists call denial. That is also a great hindrance to successful communication.

Some people, in what they believe is an act of kindness, will always tell you that you were wonderful. Don't believe them. Preachers are especially vulnerable to this danger. Christians who misunderstand their Christianity think that criticism is always a sin. So they won't tell you the truth when you have bombed.

Christianity Today recently did a study of preachers, asking them to list their strengths and weaknesses. They found that most preachers placed "preaching" on the top of their list of strengths. Now, if you have been to church lately, you know that a lot of them were either lying or denying. Don't let that happen to you.

If it is an egg, don't call it a quiche. If it is a bomb, don't call it a rocket. If you failed, own it, admit it and then do something to fix it.

Cultivate friends who love you and who will tell you the truth. After I had given a speech at a service club once, a dentist friend who was one of my closest friends leaned over and said, "Steve, you ought to put that one on the bottom of the pile." Do you know what I did? I put it on the bottom of the pile.

3. Do ameliorate the failure. Owning the failure doesn't mean that you ought not make an effort at damage control. Sometimes that damage consists of an apology to someone you have offended. Sometimes the damage control is saying to the person who invited you to speak, "Look, I'm not stupid. That was a bad speech. However, I do want you to ask me back, because I can be a lot better than I was today." Sometimes damage control calls for a letter to a person with whom you were in a horrible conversation: "I just wanted you to know that I wasn't myself yesterday. I do hope you can find it in your heart to overlook some of the dumb things I said. God isn't through with me yet."

Sometimes you can ameliorate the failure in your next speech, debate, or conversation. I have often said to my students the day after a bombed lecture, "I need to correct a possible misunderstanding of some of the things I said yesterday. What I meant was. . . ."

The point is this: After you have bombed, ask yourself if there is anything you can salvage from the ruins. If you can think of something, do it. If you can't, accept it and move ahead.

4. Do fix the failure. In the early days of plastic surgery, I'm told, there was the spurious belief that anesthetics marred the results of the plastic surgery. So, if you were ugly and wanted to be beautiful, you had a choice. You could accept the pain and make the change, or you could avoid the pain and stay ugly.

It is the same way with communication skills. Failure is painful but, if you fix what was wrong, the pain will lead to a change.

Let me sum up the pedagogical points of this chapter in the words of that great

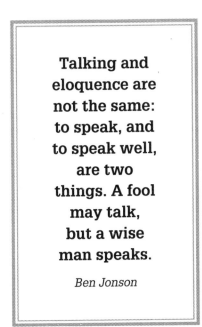

Talking and eloquence are not the same: to speak, and to speak well, are two things. A fool may talk, but a wise man speaks.

Ben Jonson

theologian and philosopher, Mary Tyler Moore: "If it doesn't hurt some, you're doing it wrong."

A Final Word (well, maybe a few final words)

Someone has said that the most miserable people in the world are not the people who didn't get what they wanted, but those who got what they wanted and found out that it wasn't really what they wanted. That is true in a lot of areas. Being single is hard, but it is not half as bad as waking up on Monday morning and finding out that one has married the wrong person. It is hard to be poor, and I make no brief for poverty, but, at least a poor person can think of how wonderful it would be to be rich. Thinking rich people always come to the horrible realization that the promise of riches didn't deliver happiness and now they are left with no hope.

Just so, don't expect that achieving effective communication skills will fill the emptiness inside or make you the kind of person you always wanted to be. You can be an effective communicator (and that's what this book is all about), but don't make that goal, and the achieving of it, carry more baggage than it was designed to carry.

There are certain things that only God can do. Only God can give ultimate meaning to what you communicate. Only God can fill the emptiness that is endemic to human nature. Only God can give an individual the positive self-image that most of us seek from other people. Augustine prayed, "Thou hast created us for Thyself, and our hearts are restless until they find their rest in Thee."

This book has been about communication. Communication is important. But life is about God, and, if you miss Him, no matter how well you communicate, you won't have anything of ultimate importance to say. That would be a tragedy.

My fear is that as you learn to communicate, you will forget to listen to God, the ultimate communicator. He has gone to a lot of trouble to communicate His message of love, acceptance, forgiveness, and eternal life.

You see . . .

Your words, no matter how eloquent
Your speeches, no matter how effective
Your conversations, no matter how stimulating
Your debates, no matter how victorious
Will all die when you die.

Then the only talking
that will be important
will be what He says to you.

Steve Brown is President and Bible teacher for Key Life Network, Inc., and professor of preaching at Reformed Theological Seminary, Orlando, Florida. His voice, humor, and insight have become familiar to thousands who listen to him daily in many cities. He is the author of numerous books and articles in magazines such as *Decision* and *Leadership*. Steve serves as one of the members of the board of directors of *Christianity Today*. An abridged version of this book is also available in audio format (0-8010-3032-3).

Also by Steve Brown

Approaching God
Born Free
If God Is in Charge
If Jesus Has Come
Jumping Hurdles
Heirs with the Price
Living Free
No More Mr. Nice Guy
Our Lord, the Holy Spirit
When Your Rope Breaks
Welcome to the Family
When Being Good Isn't Good Enough